To MOOC or Not to MOOC

Chandos

Information Professional Series

Series Editor: Ruth Rikowski
(email: Rikowskigr@aol.com)

Chandos' new series of books is aimed at the busy information professional. They have been specially commissioned to provide the reader with an authoritative view of current thinking. They are designed to provide easy-to-read and (most importantly) practical coverage of topics that are of interest to librarians and other information professionals. If you would like a full listing of current and forthcoming titles, please visit www.chandospublishing.com.

New authors: we are always pleased to receive ideas for new titles; if you would like to write a book for Chandos, please contact Dr Glyn Jones on g.jones.2@elsevier.com or telephone +44 (0) 1865 843000.

To MOOC or Not to MOOC

How Can Online Learning Help to Build the Future of Higher Education?

Sarah Porter

ELSEVIER

AMSTERDAM • BOSTON • CAMBRIDGE • HEIDELBERG
LONDON • NEW YORK • OXFORD • PARIS • SAN DIEGO
SAN FRANCISCO • SINGAPORE • SYDNEY • TOKYO
Chandos Publishing is an imprint of Elsevier

CP
CHANDOS PUBLISHING

Chandos Publishing is an imprint of Elsevier
225 Wyman Street, Waltham, MA 02451, USA
Langford Lane, Kidlington, OX5 1GB, UK

ISBN: 978-0-08-100048-9

British Library Cataloguing-in-Publication Data
A catalogue record for this book is available from the British Library

Library of Congress Cataloging-in-Publication Data
A catalog record for this book is available from the Library of Congress

For information on all Chandos Publishing publications
visit our website at http://store.elsevier.com

Acquisition Editor: Glyn Jones
Editorial Project Manager: Harriet Clayton
Production Project Manager: Preethy Simonraj
Designer: Matthew Limbert

Printed in the United States of America

Contents

List of tables

Biography

Sarah Porter is an academic visitor at the Oxford Internet Institute at the University of Oxford and an independent consultant working in higher education. Sarah's research interests are in the potential for technology to enhance education and research, particularly at a tertiary level. Her experience is gleaned from 20 years experience in researching and developing e-learning technologies, covering roles at prominent UK universities and national organizations. Most notably this involved more than 10 years leading innovation and development programs at Jisc, the UK's main body for innovation in education and research. She has presented and written widely on the issues and challenges of getting the most value from the potential of IT in an educational context and has a particular interest in the tension between strategy and opportunity that IT presents to educational organizations.

Introduction

Massive open online courses, or MOOCs as they are now commonly known, have become media buzzwords in recent years, attracting both positive and critical coverage in the mainstream press across the world, as well as many thousands of online articles, discussions, and tweets. With the arrival of MOOCs, educational technology, and its role in the future of higher education, has crossed over from the purview of academics, parents, and students to be topics that engage the public. Everyone seems to have an opinion about MOOCs and whether they hold fantastic promise for the future of higher education and are likely to open up higher education qualifications to many millions of people at low or marginal cost, or whether they are simply the latest overhyped news story and an opportunity for elite institutions to get even more press coverage than usual.

There are elements of truth in both views, but what has become increasingly clear in recent times is that the future of MOOCs is much less predictable than we might conclude from some of the press coverage. No one can say at this point whether MOOCs will fulfill the promised change to the higher education system or whether they are an educational bubble that will burst this year, next year, or the year after. It is still too early to tell if they will succeed in the goal of some of the leading MOOC platforms, to disrupt the global higher education system. With MOOCs, the future of higher education has become as difficult to predict—and vulnerable to fast-growing, disruptive newcomers—as any other industry. Higher education has for the first time become an Internet commodity and open to the same pressures that we have seen affect the music and publishing industries—and with outcomes that are just as unpredictable.

What is equally notable about this trend in technological and educational innovation is the speed at which MOOCs have been accepted by the general public as part of the educational landscape. Many universities have barely had time to understand the main MOOC systems and their early business models, and to begin to plan their own response, before other new providers are emerging and a whole range of different MOOC and business models are being discussed. One of the biggest challenges for all involved in MOOCs, including the big MOOC platforms, is to move forward at an appropriate rate of change—to keep moving fast enough to maintain momentum, but not so fast that many possible participants are left behind.

The momentum has not slowed down and whatever the commentators may believe, for the millions of MOOC students who are voting with their keyboards, MOOCs are just another part of the Internet phenomenon. Increasingly, Internet services are free, as is much of the content; online users are familiar with casually signing up to the wealth of new services, using them for a time, and then embracing the next new trend as it appears. For this type of consumer, who increasingly represents the mainstream and not just the technical expert or early adopter of technology, why should education be any different to free services such as YouTube or the BBC Web site? The "freemium" model, where most content is provided for free and other services are offered for a charge, is prevalent for online media sites such as newspapers. Consumers increasingly expect rapid change in online services, with new products and services appearing regularly, and new features and added value to those services that they already use. And they expect to be able to sample many of these services for free, at least initially, with the option to purchase 'added value' at a cost.

The more disruptive challenge to the majority of higher education institutions, which at times are like rabbits caught in the headlights of MOOCs is feeling that they need to respond to the challenge of online education, and not be "left behind" their peers, but not knowing how to react or what approach to adopt if they do decide to invest in MOOCs.

This book examines MOOC developments to date, and focuses in particular upon how a range of different universities have responded in practical terms to this phenomenon. It draws out some of the main issues that need to be considered when a university or college decides whether to engage with MOOCS or not, and gives guidance on how to respond to MOOCs now and in the future. The information in the book is based upon interviews with over 20 universities across the globe, and looks at the full range of related issues including governance and decision-making, quality assurance, costing and business models, as well as the options of working with an external MOOC platform or choosing to take an independent approach.

It is recognized that MOOCs are just part of a long-term trend toward using technology in higher education, and the recommendations are rooted in the context of the ongoing disruption that we are seeing in higher education globally, and the need for universities and colleges to plan a coherent strategy for how they map their way through it. Online technologies are only one part of this context, but a part that has the potential to support positive, planned change as well as to undermine and disrupt current models.

Why do MOOCs matter?

The higher education industry has had "an anomalously long run of disruption-free growth … (where) fundamental change has been unnecessary" (Christensen & Eyring, 2011). Even when faced with the truly disruptive potential of online technology, the university sector has failed to change. As George Siemens says: "To date, higher education has largely failed to learn the lessons of participatory culture, distributed and fragmented value systems and networked learning. MOOCs have forced a serious assessment of the idea of a university and how education should be related to and supportive of the society in which it exists" (Siemens, 2014).

Part of the problem is that despite its current trials and tribulations, demand for higher education has continued to exceed supply, the elite have been able to continue with only a little cost-cutting, and many institutions have been able to weather the storm of reduced public investment and higher levels of scrutiny.

Things are now beginning to change as costs have increased and competition from new entrants is also increasing. Online learning is a disruptive technology that is allowing for-profit and not-for-profit institutions—and other suppliers, such as publishers, software companies, training providers—to apply fresh thinking the higher education model, considering options such as "unbundling" (Rizvi, Donnelly, & Barber, 2013) where the higher education lifecycle might be segmented and delivered in new ways. At the same time, consumers of higher education are being much more circumspect about the "product" of a university, constantly increasing their demand to understand exactly what they are choosing and, ultimately, paying for.

MOOCs are the latest step in the development of the disruptive online learning technology continuum. Although the systems that are used in MOOCs may not be particularly new or advanced from a technical perspective—at least at this stage in their development—the scale at which they are being used, with class sizes typically in the thousands, and the large numbers of institutions that are investing significant resources and reputation in them, mean that they are having a marked impact on how we think about higher education.

That said, online learning technologies have been around for a long time and so far, many institutions have been able to resist anything more than selective dabbling with them. Some technologies, such as virtual learning environments or learning management systems, have become prevalent in the sector, but it has been a long and slow journey to reach the current point of usage, and in most institutions, the deployment is simple and fails to challenge face-to-face teaching, other than in small pockets of innovative teaching. The higher education market has proven to be remarkably resistant to the disruptive potential of online learning.

This can be partly explained by the unique position that the whole higher education sector holds when compared to other markets, as described by Clayton Christensen, the creator of the theory of disruptive innovation:

> *… universities are an anomaly that my original framing of disruption could not explain. … the demise of incumbents that characterizes most industries in the late stages of disruption has rarely occurred among colleges and universities. We have had entry, but not exit*
>
> *Christensen & Eyring (2011)*

According to Christensen and Eyring, three characteristics of higher education have led to this situation:

- Teaching—this has been difficult to disrupt because "its human qualities could not be replicated"—but this will change in a technological environment where there is a shift from the individual teacher or institution to what the learner will learn (and how).
- Two kinds of students, some of whom want the traditional campus experience, so are difficult to disrupt—though those for whom the traditional campus-based model does not work because of the context in which they operate, may be classic disruptors.
- Alumni and funders—their strong affiliation to an institution is often based on a personal relationship and this gives "staying power unique to higher education" (Christensen & Eyring, 2011).

Some institutions may be able to continue to ride out the storm, drawing upon the strengths of their reputation and their relationships with alumni and funders. For many others, though, there are opportunities afforded by learning technologies that are now too significant to be ignored. Not only can online learning open up the institution to a global market on a previously unprecedented scale, potentially both the quantity and quality of potential students at all levels of study, but the new approaches that are afforded mean that universities can position themselves at the cutting edge of the right type of teaching and, more importantly, the learning experience. Universities can demonstrate that they are true innovators in practice and not just in theory.

This is not to say that MOOCs in their current form are perfect examples of innovative technology, nor that all MOOC ventures are successful. The short history of MOOCs to date has shown that we should not rush to make assumptions about who MOOC students are likely to be, what they most want from MOOCs, or their motivation for learning online. All the more reason, we would argue, that now is the right time for universities to commit to informed experimentation with MOOCs and other online learning approaches, in order to equip themselves for the journey of adaptation and disruption that lies ahead. Institutions should make their own decisions about how they engage with online learning, and these decisions need to be informed by their own context, strategy, and experience. Universities will best equip themselves for their future strategies by experimenting with MOOCs and other online educational tools, and learning from this about what is possible and what best suits their needs and priorities.

Ernst and Young (2012) provide a helpful categorization of the reasons why a university might want to engage with MOOCs:

- Defensive—to be ready if/when MOOCs (online learning) take off.
- Offensive—to become a leader in online learning.
- Marketing—to market the university, for example, to translate free access MOOC students into paying students, or to reach international students.
- Enhance existing provision—to provide blended learning for existing students, for example, to develop online components for existing courses.
- Change existing provision—to focus more teaching time on two-way learning conversations with students rather than one-way lecturing: the so-called "flipped classroom."
- Financial—to reduce teaching costs and hence the price to students.
- Research—to explore MOOCs/online learning in practice and in greater depth and become a leader in MOOC research.

All of these possible motivations are explored through this book, which examines new research to look at why universities and colleges are engaging with MOOCs, or are not. The research undertaken reveals that in many cases, an institution will be driven by more than one of the motivating factors, and is often interested in exploring many of them at the same time. This is understandable, but can lead to a situation where there are multiple strategic drivers that are being explored at the same time, and it can be difficult for the university to identify how successful the experiment has been in achieving its objectives. For this reason, this book focuses upon institutional strategy and the need to focus clearly upon it when planning the strategy for online learning and MOOCs.

Finally, although this work focuses on MOOCs and online learning in particular, the intention is that it should be read within a context of understanding the priorities and motivation of each unique institution. The more nuanced theory of higher education that is proposed by Christensen is that online learning may be a "sustaining innovation" that will work alongside traditional campuses and face-to-face teaching to strengthen universities and colleges. Those institutions that are able to adapt to, and embrace, the new technologies will be best placed to continue with what is excellent and special about what they do already, while taking best advantage of what is new.

References

Christensen, C., & Eyring, H. J. (2011). *The innovative university*. San Francisco: Jossey-Bass.

Ernst and Young. (2012). *University of the future*. Ernst and Young, Online at http://www.ey.com/Publication/vwLUAssets/University_of_the_future/$FILE/University_of_the_Future_2012.pdf.

Rizvi, S., Donnelly, K., & Barber, M. (2013). *An avalanche is coming. Higher education and the revolution ahead*. Institute for Public Policy Research, Online at http://www.ippr.org/publications/an-avalanche-is-coming-higher-education-and-the-revolution-ahead.

Siemens, G. (2014). *The attack on our higher education system – and why we should welcome it*, Online at http://blog.ted.com/2014/01/31/the-attack-on-our-higher-education-system-and-why-we-should-welcome-it/.

Part One

What are MOOCs?

1

Introduction

Definitions for MOOCs (Massive Open Online Courses) and other forms of online learning, the history of MOOCs, how they were first developed by George Siemens and Stephen Downes and how they have evolved since have been described in this chapter. Before examining the short history of MOOCs and discussing their evolution, it is useful to understand what exactly a MOOC is and what makes it different to similar systems, in particular online learning and open educational resources (OER).

Definitions

MOOCs are about 7 years old, though it is only in the last 3 years that they have achieved a widespread, global, profile. MOOCs have arisen from a long continuum of experimentation with educational technology and online learning, and with pedagogic approaches that are made possible through technology. And as with a small number of other technological innovations, the results have then been replicated many times since to create an established and well-understood model that is being used world wide.

There is no shortage of new terminology and acronyms in the field of educational technology, and many of the terms are used interchangeably, or with subtly different meanings.

The most commonly used terminology that is relevant to MOOCs is summarized below:

- Technology-enhanced learning or e-learning: any technology that is used to support a learning experience. This may or may not use the Internet, so electronic white boards and interactive polling systems are both forms of e-learning technologies, as well as learning systems such as virtual learning environments or learning management systems, that rely upon Internet technologies in order to deliver content and connect learners together.
- Online learning: learning that takes place online using Internet technologies. It will rely upon e-learning systems in many cases.
- Open educational resources: digital content that is licensed so that it can be used for educational purposes by others than the content owner. Licenses vary and may be broad and inclusive or more narrowly defined, for example, only allowing not-for-profit use of the resources. OER are also supported by an international movement that aims to make increasing amounts of digital content available for free, public use.
- MOOC: a specific online course that is openly available to unlimited numbers of participants, free of charge. It is also a form of online learning and MOOCs use educational technology in order to function. They may also use OER as their main source of content.

MOOCs have the following characteristics:

- **Massive:** MOOCs are intended to be run at scale, with hundreds or even thousands of participants and without any limit to student numbers being imposed.
- **Open:** MOOCs are intended to be open—with the word "open" used to imply that access to MOOC is both free of charge and also that access to MOOCs is unrestricted. MOOCs have no entry requirements and are open to learners of all educational background, age, and location.
- **Online:** MOOCs are delivered completely online and involve no face-to-face contact. They are delivered through Internet technologies and so make it easy for students to communicate with each other while learning and for students to access resources that are available elsewhere on the web.
- **Course:** One of the key attributes that differentiates MOOCs from an open educational resource is that they have the characteristics of a traditional course—they are run during a specific time period, based upon prescribed content, and instruction is provided to the student during that period of time. As with traditional courses, there is also usually an element of assessment included in MOOC, and this may include some form of accreditation (which is a thorny topic and one to which we will return later on).

MOOC terminology

Through this work, we will use some MOOC terminology regularly. We will define these terms here in order to be clear about the differences between each of them.

MOOC(s): The individual online courses that are made available for anyone to study.

MOOC platforms: The branded online systems that are used to host MOOC courses.

Coursera, EdX, Udacity, and FutureLearn are some of the best known at present.

MOOC providers: The universities or other organizations that create the MOOC courses and, in most cases, provide teaching and learning support to MOOC students through the online platform.

Even in their short history of development, MOOCs have already diversified into other models, for example, MOOCs which are aimed at smaller groups of learners and are usually available to a limited group of people, and not open to the general public; these are being called Small Private Online Courses. As the MOOCosphere develops and changes very quickly, many other new models and approaches will be developed, with varied models for learning, teaching, and delivery, and different underlying business models. The future sustainability of MOOCs as a model of higher education depends largely upon developing models that have the right combination of learners, delivery, and business model. We will discuss some of the different MOOC models in the case studies and also analyze their respective pros and cons in the final chapters of the book.

Where did MOOCs come from?

This section briefly describes the genesis of the MOOC phenomenon. The first course labeled as an MOOC was created and taught by George Siemens and Stephen Downes, two well-known pioneers of online learning working in Canada. Siemens and Downes share an interest in education and models of learning, with particular affiliation to a theory of learning called connectivism. Siemens is a leading academic working with this theory, while Stephen Downes in particular had long experience of working at the cutting edge of e-learning practice, leading initiatives in OER, personalized learning, and other areas, and is a respected commentator on some of the most challenging topics of the future of online education.

In 2008, the team taught a traditional, fee-paying course to 25 students at the University of Manitoba but also made the radical and far-sighted decision to open up access to the course to anyone who wished to join it online. About 2200 people joined the students on the course. The course topic was Connectivism and Connective Knowledge, connectivism being an educational theory that emphasizes the importance of connections between people and knowledge. The Internet and social media allow new possibilities for exploring connectivist approaches, as they enable communication between very large groups of people to happen quickly and easily, so the subject matter was ideally suited for the experiment that was to take place.

The hope and expectation of Siemens and Downes was that by opening up the course to a much wider and nonselective group of students, it would provide a rich and fertile ground on which to test out connectivism in practice, bringing together a small cohort of students following a formal educational route with a much larger and more diverse group of interested individuals.

So did it work? It was clearly a fascinating experiment and it comes to life as we read Downes' updates on his experience of teaching the course (Downes, 2008) and subsequent reflections by Siemens and others (Fini, 2009). Downes muses upon the student responses to the course materials, which included weekly videos of himself and others, live discussions sessions (run twice in order to cope with the range of time zones in which students were based), an online discussion forum, and the overall course delivery system, which he adapted from his online newsletter system. Like many ground-breaking initiatives in online learning, this was a live and raw experiment where the teachers had to wrestle with technical systems to "bend" them to work how they wanted and had to carry out their own administration—registering students online in batches—as well as creating digital course materials just days or sometimes hours before they went live.

Some years after the course was taught, it is still considered to have been a success on two levels. First, as an approach to learning and teaching with a large cohort of distributed students, it proved itself to be successful: the use of the digital medium made it easy to gather data about how students interacted with the course content and their level of contribution to class discussion and other activity, such as writing blog posts. The data revealed that students were contributing to discussions, creating content, and engaging with their peers.

Second, the experiment has been considered by many commentators as a successful example of both a different way to construct a course with a much broader cohort and a new philosophical approach to the way that higher education courses are structured and delivered. It is the seed that was sown through this single experiment that has led to the fervor and strong opinions about MOOCs in the last 2 years.

Siemens, Downes, and others spent time and effort reflecting upon their experiences and attempting to describe the theoretical distinctions of their model. In doing this, they coined the terms cMOOC (connectivist) and xMOOC (traditional, see below). cMOOC is exemplified by the original MOOC that was run in 2008; a cMOOC is taught according to connectivist principles, combining open learning with distributed content. The connectivist network is at the heart of a cMOOC; it may be offered outside a traditional academic institution by a network of interested and specialist individuals, and the student has a lot of autonomy to govern their own interaction with the course and its content, choosing the content that they wish to interact with and the nature of their own participation.

About 2 years after this first MOOC ran, parallel activities were taking place at some of the leading institutions in the United States that would converge with the MOOC experiment to create the phenomenon that we see today.

Daphne Koller and Andrew Ng were both teaching traditional courses in Computer Science at Stanford University and wished to introduce elements of educational technology in order to improve the learning experience for the students (Leber, 2012). They began to experiment with what is now known as the "flipped classroom" model, where traditional, campus-based students use educational technology resources such as online lectures and digitized experiments to prepare for their classes in advance, and use the face-to-face time for deeper interaction with their peer group and teachers. At the same time, Sebastian Thrun, who also taught at Stanford, was carrying out an experiment in online teaching similar to the much earlier Siemens and Downes experiment, but which was making news by attracting some hundreds of thousands of online students.

Learning from these separate experiments converged together and the terminology developed by Siemens and Downes was adopted more widely to give a name to what was seen as an exciting experiment that promised (or threatened) to subvert the traditional models of higher education.

xMOOC

The MOOCs with which we are most familiar today, and which we might describe as traditional MOOCs, are a form of xMOOCs. These are MOOCs that follow a more traditional structure and delivery approach, are probably offered by a recognized academic institution, and are where the course is highly structured and with clear expectations for how the student will engage with the course (see Table 1.1 for more details about the two types of MOOCs).

It is useful to understand the terminology and the part that they plan in the genesis of the MOOC. However, the boundaries between the two types of MOOCs are

Table 1.1 The attributes of xMOOCs and cMOOCs

xMOOCs		cMOOCs
Scalability of provision	Massive	Community and connections
Open access—restricted license	Open	Open access and license
Individual learning in single platform	Online	Networked learning across multiple platforms and services
Acquire a curriculum of knowledge and skills	Course	Develop shared practices, knowledge, and understanding

Yuan, Powell, and Olivier (2014).

becoming increasingly blurred as more MOOCs are developed, and as new types of MOOC emerge that include characteristics of both types. xMOOCs or cMOOCs will not be referred to specifically through this work, instead as is the norm, generic term MOOC will be used to mean both.

The growth of MOOCs

So we can see that although MOOCs seem to have come out of nowhere, MOOCs have their own short history, which builds upon and is rooted in much longer term research and development in online learning, learning content, and trends such as open education, and investment by both public and private organizations in developing new online learning tools and courses.

MOOCs are thus the latest step in a global trend of growth in online learning. This is seen in all parts of the world, both developing and developed. The Sloan Consortium survey of online learning in the US (Sloan, 2013) shows growth from 1.6 million online students in the US in 2002 to 7.1 million in 2013.

At the same time, attitudes to online learning by university management are increasingly positive; also cited in the Sloan report, the percentage of academic leaders rating the learning outcomes in online education as the same or superior to those as in face-to-face instruction, grew from 57% in 2003 to 74% in 2013. In the US, online courses have become part of the fabric of higher education, with 61% of liberal arts colleges offering some online courses (Parker, Lenhart, & Moore, 2011).

When we come to look at MOOCs, we see a remarkable growth in the numbers of courses provided and the numbers of MOOC students since large-scale MOOCs began in 2011. At the time of writing, in April 2014, there are 2230 MOOCs available, growing at an astonishing rate from just 409 MOOCs in March 2013, with a particularly large increase in new courses being launched in early 2014, as growing numbers of organizations committed to joining the MOOC market (Open Education Europa, 2014).

We do not know exactly how many people have signed up for MOOCs but even a conservative estimate, based solely upon the students registered with the "big three" platforms, Coursera, EdX, and Udacity, puts the number of registered MOOC students at over 8.5 million (Blake, 2014). These figures are increasing every day as the awareness of MOOCs spreads beyond the early adopter community, of the tech-savvy individuals, to the broader community of learners, with particularly strong growth outside the western world (Blake, 2014).

Criticism of MOOCs

As we can see from the figures above, many millions of people have so far signed up for MOOCs. MOOC completion rates are not so encouraging, however, this being one of the main criticisms made of MOOCs, particularly where they have been seen to suggest that they offer an alternative to formal higher education. It is useful to look at the data behind the impressive MOOC recruitment figures in order to understand the reality a little better.

Completion rates for the large-scale MOOCs, such as Coursera and EdX, are typically less than 13% of those who registered for the course before it started, with many MOOCs seeing completion rates as low as 4% or 5% (Jordan, 2014).

Taking one particular institution as an example, the University of Edinburgh had over 300,000 students registered for the six Edinburgh MOOCs that were run in 2013. Statements of Accomplishment (which indicate that the learner has viewed most or all of the MOOC content) were issued to only 12% of those who initially registered to take the MOOC—a still impressive 30,000 students, but considerably less than those who had originally registered to take the MOOC.

If we equate a learner who registers for an MOOC with one who registers for a traditional university course, these statistics appear to be fairly damning. However, there is much debate about how to calculate completion rates for MOOCs. MOOC providers and researchers alike have pointed out that looking at numbers of those who register for an MOOC, before the MOOC starts, may not be the best way to make a realistic prediction for active MOOC students. For example, for the student numbers given above, the University of Edinburgh discounts all those who registered for the MOOC but did not access the first week of the course. They use as their starting point the concept of "active learners," that is those who make an actual commitment of time to start to study the MOOC, rather than anyone who registers for an MOOC. When this definition of an active learner is used, then the completion figures are 21% (MOOCs@Edinburgh Group, 2013); and for some other MOOCs, completion rates have been as high as nearly 50% (Jordan, 2014).

However, we choose to analyze them, the completion figures for MOOCs to date do not compare in any way with the completion figures for traditional higher education courses, and this seems to substantiate one of the main criticisms of MOOCs—namely, that many people sign up for them but few complete them.

This is, though, using the wrong comparators for MOOCs. We should not compare the motivation of someone who signs up to a free, online course with that of someone who commits substantial financial and personal resources to a traditional higher education course. It is not realistic to expect all those who register initially for an MOOC to take any of the course, let alone all of it. We need to think again about the expectations and priorities of the target audience of learners before we seek to analyze the statistics for completion and try to understand the motivation of the learners. This is clearly a very complex issue, and made even more so when we see that completion rates for individual MOOCs can vary widely—in the Edinburgh case, "with ranges of 4–44% and 2–36%, respectively, across the individual courses" (MOOCs@Edinburgh Group, 2013). We will return to this issue in later chapters.

References

Blake, D. (2014). *MOOC infographic, January 9, 2014. MOOCS.com*. Online at http://moocs.com/index.php/category/mooc-infographics/.

Downes, S. (2008). *The Daily, September 08, 2008. Connectivism and connective knowledge*. Online at http://connect.downes.ca/archive/08/09_08_thedaily.htm.

Fini, A. (2009). The technological dimension of a massive open online course: the case of the CCK08 course tools. *International Review of Research in Open and Distance Learning, 10*(5). Online at http://www.irrodl.org/index.php/irrodl/article/view/643/1402.

Jordan, K. (2014). *MOOC completion rates: the data.* Katy Jordan, researching education and technology, Online at http://www.katyjordan.com/MOOCproject.html.

Leber, J. (2012). *The Technology of Massive Open Online Courses.* MIT Technology Review. Online at http://www.technologyreview.com/news/506326/the_technology_of_massive_open_online_courses/.

MOOCs@Edinburgh Group. (2013). *MOOCs @ Edinburgh 2013: Report #1.* University of Edinburgh, Online at https://www.era.lib.ed.ac.uk/handle/1842/6683.

Open Education Europa. (2014). *European MOOCs scoreboard.* European Commission, Online at http://www.openeducationeuropa.eu/en/european_scoreboard_moocs.

Parker, K., Lenhart, A., & Moore, K. (2011). *The digital revolution and higher education.* Pew Research Center, Online at http://www.pewinternet.org/2011/08/28/the-digital-revolution-and-higher-education/.

Sloan Foundation. (2013). *Grade change: Online education in the United States, 2013.* Sloan Foundation, Online at http://sloanconsortium.org/publications/survey/grade-change-2013.

Yuan, L., Powell, S., & Olivier, W. (2014). *Beyond MOOCs: Sustainable online learning in institutions.* Centre for Educational Technology, Interoperability and Standards, Online at http://publications.cetis.ac.uk/2014/898.

The MOOCosphere

2

Introduction

Within 2 years, the market of key Massive Online Open Course (MOOC) players has developed and achieved worldwide recognition. The current main MOOC providers are Coursera, EdX, and Udacity. Each of these three organizations has its own history and it is useful to understand that they vary quite considerably in philosophy and approach—even at this early stage on their development path.

Although US led, these players have all very quickly connected with institutions around the world and have built networks of MOOC providers that stretch across the globe as truly international organizations. Institutions in Europe and Australasia have been particularly quick to sign up with the "big three," there is now also a substantial number of partners across the world and MOOCs are being offered by many different providers in many different languages.

Before we go further, let us briefly describe the three most prominent providers and explore their history and current market share.

Coursera

Coursera emerged from the Department of Computer Science at Stanford University where Nancy Koller and Andrew Ng were experimenting with using online technologies to enhance traditional teaching and became interested in the potential to use the tools that they were developing to reach a much larger audience (Koller, 2013).

Of the MOOC platforms, Coursera has achieved the most publicity and grown most quickly. Precise figures change (increase) daily but at the time of writing, Coursera had over 8 million "students," 107 partners and offers over 600 courses (Coursera, 2015). This is bigger than any of the competitors by many multipliers. The reason for this is probably due to Coursera's very active and focused growth strategy, where it has targeted its recruitment of partners upon the top tier institutions in many countries across the world and been able to accommodate a fast-growing number of new partners and courses. Although it has emerged from an academic institution, it has quickly established itself as a successful "start-up" with the characteristics that go along with that: clear and ambitious growth strategies; fast recruitment of team members who will pursue partners and "customers"; significant investment that supports fast growth. We will explore further later on the issue of the lineage or "DNA" of a particular venture and what that can mean to those who engage with it.

Udacity

Udacity was launched in 2012 after Sebastian Thrun, its founder, experimented with offering free, open access to some of his Stanford University computer science classes. These classes were astonishingly successful—160,000 students registered for them—and this success led Thrun and colleagues to quickly seek investment from venture capitalists to establish a for-profit company that would offer MOOCs across a range of subject areas, with particular emphasis on formal qualifications in technical subject areas, such as software development. In early 2014, Udacity was offering 28 courses and had registered about a million students (Udacity, 2014a).

Particularly notable and much reported is its partnership with Georgia Tech University: Udacity and Georgia Tech together have offered a new MSc course in Computer Science, with a fee level of US$ 6600, many times lower than the on campus cost of US$ 46,000. This radical experiment is currently underway, though at the time of writing it has been "suspended" by the college administration, who deny that this is due to the lower achievement rates of the MOOC-track students when compared with traditional students (Kolowich, 2013). Whatever the final outcome, the experience will inform the ongoing development of the Udacity business model, which holds potential for sustainability in ways that some other models do not.

Udacity has grown less quickly than its main competitors, partly because its model is slightly different: it has focused upon working with a small group of partners rather than recruiting many universities as partners. In fact, it has now diversified further: in late 2013 it made public statements about a change of direction for the company and established the Open Education Alliance which aims to "bridge the gap between the skills employers need and what traditional universities teach." The Alliance includes members from the corporate sector that have particular skills gaps, including Google and AT&T. Udacity's explicit focus is upon "reducing the skills gap through education" (Udacity, 2014b). So it seems likely that for the medium-term future, other than working with a handful of technically focused universities, Udacity has chosen to refocus its strategy away from traditional higher education and, as such, will be less relevant to our discussion here.

We will return to the issue of business models and accreditation later on as these are probably the most challenging and unclear factors for MOOCs at present—and that will impact upon whether MOOCs become established as a viable and normal addition to traditional higher education, remain marginal, or disappear entirely.

EdX

EdX has a different lineage to Udacity and Coursera. Like them, it has emerged from the elite university sector in the United States, but unlike the others, it has been established from the start as a not-for-profit venture and its initial investment has come from commitment by its two sponsoring organizations, MIT and Harvard, rather than from venture capital. Each of the two sponsoring universities has invested US$ 30 million.

EdX was originally started at MIT and was known for a short period as MITx, until Harvard also became involved and a new brand was established. As MITx, it built upon a long history (in Internet terms) of experimentation with educational technology and commitment to principles of open sharing and open source, going back to the MIT Open CourseWare Initiative (OCW) that was started in 2001 (MIT, 2014), with strong institutional support from the University, and which has been a global leader in free, online materials. As such, OCW is an important and influential forerunner to MOOCs and has clearly influenced the development of EdX and its ongoing ethos and approach, while also having a broader impact upon numerous other initiatives and projects worldwide, including the many Open Educational Resource programs.

EdX has grown quickly in both numbers of courses offered and also in student numbers registered. It has about 30 partners, with just over a half of the partners institutions in North America and the other partners are institutions across the globe, including several each in Asia and Europe. EdX currently offers 91 courses across a wide range of disciplines (EdX, 2014). Most courses are offered in English but there are some in Mandarin, French, and other languages.

As a nonprofit venture, EdX clearly has different financial ambitions from its main competitors. However, it still needs to generate income in order to cover its costs, and to continue to grow. As with Udacity and Coursera, EdX is testing out different approaches to developing its suite of courses and generating revenue. Unlike the other main platforms, EdX has announced its intention to make the technology, behind its platform, available free as open source software, called "OpenEdX" (Meyer, 2013).

However, it will also provide charged-for services for those who are using the platform as a delivery mechanism for their own courses. EdX is also offering a range of paid-for services to its partners. It works with partners to create courses, with the current price set at US$ 200,000 per course, and EdX taking a share of the profits when the course is run (though this assumes that there will be profits; in these early days of MOOC development, this is by no means certain or even likely).

Developments in Europe

In mainland Europe, there are many MOOC consortia and partnerships that have been established and others are under development. Some are Europe-wide in their focus, such as OpenUpEd (OpenUpEd, 2014), a not-for-profit platform that is run by a European consortium of open and distance-learning universities, EADTU, and funded by the European Commission. There is also Iversity, again a not-for-profit MOOC platform which is funded by a number of different partners and which uniquely offers credit for MOOCs under the European Credit Transfer System (Iversity, 2014).

In addition to this, however, is a myriad of different national MOOC platforms and schemes that are spread across the whole continent and provide MOOCs in a wide range of subject areas and different languages. Europe now provides about 500 different MOOCs, with more appearing every week. The European Scoreboard provides fascinating data about current MOOCs and also maps out the breakneck speed of growth at which new courses are being created, with a particular spurt of growth across the globe in early 2014 (OpenEuropa, 2014).

The MOOC picture in Europe is not only about courses; there is a lot of investment also in open platforms and tool sets. European institutions are building on their long-term commitment to open education, and the experience of many public open and distance-learning institutions, to share tools, technology, and good practice. One interesting example is Eliademy, from Finland (Eliademy, 2014), a free and open web and mobile platform that can be used by schools and colleges to create their own online courses, rather than acting as a content host and provider.

In December 2012, the UK's Open University, the most successful distance-learning university in the world, established the first significant European MOOC venture by announcing the establishment of FutureLearn (Open University, 2012). This is a for-profit company that is wholly owned by the Open University and which was established as a European alternative to the MOOC market dominated by North American institutions, though has also more recently branched out to include prestigious institutions from Asia and Australasia. Like its US counterparts, FutureLearn set out a very clear strategy of focusing upon the top tier institutions as its initial partners, and systematically targeted members of the research-intensive Russell Group member institutions in its first wave, so that it was able to announce 12 elite institutions as partners when it made its first announcement. Again, like its US competitors, FutureLearn carefully managed the communication around its launch so that little information had leaked out to the nonpartners in advance of the announcement, in order to make maximum impact. Its launch raised as many questions as it answered, as any detailed information about how FutureLearn would operate, what platform it would use, its business models and growth strategies, was not made available publically. It was perhaps symptomatic of the MOOC awareness at the time that many of the top—and oldest—universities in the UK were willing to publically declare their partnership with a company that although backed by a well-respected and well-established organization, in itself was a brand new venture and had only just been created. Its values, principles, and ethos were not known, and perhaps most importantly, its ability to deliver a complex and demanding new product—under intense international scrutiny—was unproven.

It seems that the decision-making process in the FutureLearn partner institutions led them to conclude that although there was risk involved, it was a calculated one, and perhaps it was less risky to be involved rather than excluded. It is also possible that these UK universities were being faced with hype about MOOCs and pressurized by senior managers and perhaps by governors to "state their position" with regard to MOOCs—were they in or out? Who were they going to work with? Or would they/should they go it alone? FutureLearn seemed to provide a relatively safe opportunity to outsource some of the experimentation and innovation to another organization, thus protecting the core business of the institution from difficult decision making and potential upheaval. FutureLearn partners are invited to join rather than to apply and, as such, are part of an exclusive "club"—a situation which also inspires comfort and confidence with universities who are used to working within the context of the UK higher education system.

FutureLearn is now up and running successfully, a new technical platform has been developed, business models are in place, including certification and processes for formal examination through a third-party company, partners are generally happy with progress and have together created a portfolio of over 70 MOOCs that give access to many of the UK's, Ireland's, and Australasia's top universities, and most recently has also attracted other partners from high calibre institutions across the world, including China and Korea. In terms of establishing a successful set of partnerships and building and delivering courses, FutureLearn is already a success, lack of established business models notwithstanding.

Evidence from FutureLearn partners indicates healthy levels of sign up for many of its MOOCs, even if they are not attracting the huge numbers that were seen in the early MOOCs (Parr, 2014). It will be interesting to see if it is able to compete with the major US players—particularly when it comes to attracting students from non-European countries. Evidence so far indicates that, perhaps against common wisdom, most students are less concerned about which university is providing the MOOC than the subject material and whether the timescales work for them. So the breadth and quality of the FutureLearn courses, underpinned by the high caliber of its partners, may be enough to sustain it as a serious contendor for global MOOC status, beyond its start-up phase. As for all the MOOC platforms, though, sustainable business models are going to be the greatest challenge. We will return to this issue in later chapters.

Other MOOC providers

Other platforms, providers, and models are emerging almost daily in the great MOOC race—and not only from within the higher education system. MOOCs have captured the attention and imagination of a very wide range of sectors and industries, ranging from charities and nongovernmental organizations to the private training sector and many spheres of business. MOOCs tap into the most current online trends in technology and user behavior, so it is not surprising that many others are wondering if there is potential for them to also explore the potential of offering online learning through the MOOC model—not least to explore its promotional and marketing potential.

In a recent article, Deloitte characterized three main ways that the corporate world may engage with MOOCs: "corporate learning (a $70 billion market), recruiting (also a $70 billion market), and even digital marketing (a $50 billion market)" (Deloitte, 2013). It will be fascinating to see how this potential for using the MOOC model in the corporate world becomes reality over the coming months and years, and whether the experimentation in the corporate world is able to shed light on some of the questions around sustainable business models that are perplexing many of the leading thinkers in higher education.

Notes

1. Although established as a European platform, FutureLearn includes partners from outside Europe, in particular prestigious institutions in Asia and Australasia.

References

Coursera. (2015). *Our mission*. Coursera, Online at https://www.coursera.org/.

Deloitte. (2013). *Signals for strategists: MOOCs teach corporations about new opportunities*. DeloitteUniversityPress,Onlineathttp://deloitte.wsj.com/riskandcompliance/files/2014/03/MOOC_report.pdf.

EdX. (2014). *EdX*. EdX, Online at https://www.edx.org/course-list/allschools/allsubjects/allcourses.

Eliademy. (2014). *Eliademy*. Eliademy, Online at https://eliademy.com.

Iversity. (2014). *About us*. Iversity, Online at https://iversity.org/en/pages/about.

Koller, N. (2013). *What we're learning from online education*. TED Conferences LLC, Online at http://www.ted.com/talks/daphne_koller_what_we_re_learning_from_online_education.

Kolowich, S. (2013). *San Jose state U. Puts MOOC project with Udacity on hold*. The Chronicle of Higher Education. http://chronicle.com/article/San-Jose-State-U-Puts-MOOC/140459/.

Meyer, R. (2013). *Harvard and MIT's online education startup has a new way to make money*. The Atlantic, Online at http://www.theatlantic.com/technology/archive/2013/10/harvard-and-mits-online-education-startup-has-a-new-way-to-make-money/280700.

MIT. (2014). *MIT open courseware*. Massachusetts Institute of Technology, Online at http://ocw.mit.edu/index.htm.

Open Education Europa. (2014). *European MOOCs scoreboard*. European Commission, Online at http://www.openeducationeuropa.eu/en/european_scoreboard_moocs.

Open University. (2012). *UK universities embrace the free, open, online future of higher education powered by the Open University*. Open University, Online at http://www3.open.ac.uk/media/fullstory.aspx?id=24794.

OpenUpEd. (2014). *OpenUpEd*. OpenUpEd, Online at http://www.openuped.eu.

Parr, C. (2014). *FutureLearn 'delighted' at response to first MOOCs*. Times Higher Education, Online at http://www.timeshighereducation.co.uk/news/futurelearn-delighted-at-response-to-first-moocs/2014010.article.

Udacity. (2014a). *About us*. Udacity, Online at https://www.udacity.com/us.

Udacity. (2014b). *Open educational alliance: create the workforce of tomorrow*. Udacity, Online at https://www.udacity.com/open-ed.

Examples of MOOCs

3

Introduction

Now that we have developed an understanding of the background to this area, the scale of the MOOCs that are available, and the platforms that people are using, it is useful to analyze some specific MOOCs—the actual courses rather than the platform—to address the question:

How do different MOOCs vary from one another, and why have they been designed in a particular way?

This section provides an overview of some of the more innovative MOOCs that are being offered to students and analyzes their characteristics, in order to illustrate some of the options for the types of MOOCs that might be offered by universities that wish to create new MOOCs, beyond the standard model of video lectures, assessments, and online social spaces.

MOOCs are at such an early stage of development that there is not yet an agreed or preferred way to describe their approach. The original taxonomy of MOOCs, as noted earlier, focused upon the distinction between an xMOOC (traditional) or cMOOC (connectivist), but this distinction is of only limited use when we wish to understand the broad range of MOOC development that is underway. While some MOOCs are following a consistent and specific design approach, often those that are hosted by the larger MOOC platforms, of video lectures, online discussion, automated assignment and peer grading, others are experimenting with many different approaches to online learning. This reflects the diversity of teaching approaches that are being used when applying educational technology in a wide range of different contexts, and the lack of clear evidence at the present time of what works best to achieve good outcomes for learners (Bowen, 2013).

So we will go beyond the xMOOC and cMOOC distinction by using a framework to guide our analysis and description. This is the "Framework for the design and evaluation of MOOCs" that has been developed in the Lytics Lab at Stanford University (http://lytics.stanford.edu/wordpress/wp-content/uploads/2013/04/Framework-for-Design-Evaluation-of-MOOCs-Grover-Franz-Schneider-Pea_final.pdf).

This framework provides a model to describe the context in which the MOOC is being designed, run, and evaluated. It is useful because it gives us a sense of the range of factors that are involved in designing and running the MOOC.

It has four main components: learner background and intentions; technology infrastructure; interactive learning environment (ILE); and evidence-based improvement.

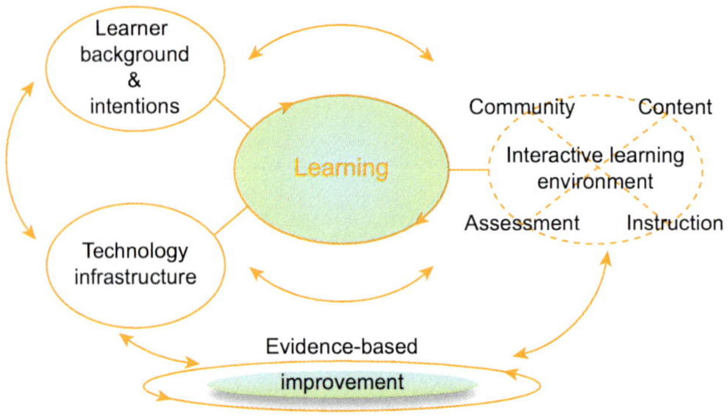

Framework for the design and evaluation of MOOCs (Grover et al., 2013)

"The *ILE* is made up of the core course elements—*Content*, *Instruction* (or Pedagogy), *Assessment*, and *Community*. These elements are initially shaped by the course creators as well as the technical affordances of the course platform. These design choices reflect the assumptions of designers about the ways in which people learn, and should be pushed to reflect the state of the art of knowledge in the learning sciences…

"*Learner background and intention* captures the variety of learner purposes for course engagement, which is a by-product of the open access nature of the courses and the novelty of the medium. Based on surveys we have conducted in some MOOCs, in addition to traditional students taking the course for some form of credit, a large percentage of others are enrolled with purposes as assorted as "curiosity about the topic," "to sharpen my job skills," and "fun and challenge." This pattern implies a need to serve up different courses suited to the varied purposes of MOOC learners: a customized learning approach that could be enabled by analytics on behavioral data from learners, as well as self-reported intentions for MOOC enrollment…

"The *technology infrastructure* comprising the MOOC platform used in conjunction with social media and other technology tools for augmenting communication and interaction powers the MOOC as a whole including its learning analytics engine, and serves to cater to diverse learner needs ranging from geography and language to issues of how the MOOC content is accessed and interacted with (e.g., downloading vs streaming video)…

"*Evidence-based improvement* is a meta-MOOC process strengthening design decisions around the ILE and technology infrastructure. Evidence-based improvement is powered by data mining and analytics designed to measure the desired course learning outcomes, and incorporates qualitative evidence from sources like forums and surveys (Grover et al., 2013)."

Below we apply the Lytics framework to four different MOOCs in order to explain how each MOOC is designed and to highlight the key characteristics of each. We look at three MOOCs that are not what may be seen as a "typical" design for traditional MOOC, and then look at more traditional xMOOC. We will see that each MOOC has been designed to meet the needs of particular learners; the chapter examines how this has been done. We recommend that readers consider sampling these or other MOOCs in order to better inform their decisions about which MOOCs to create.

Digital storytelling, DS106, University of Mary Washington

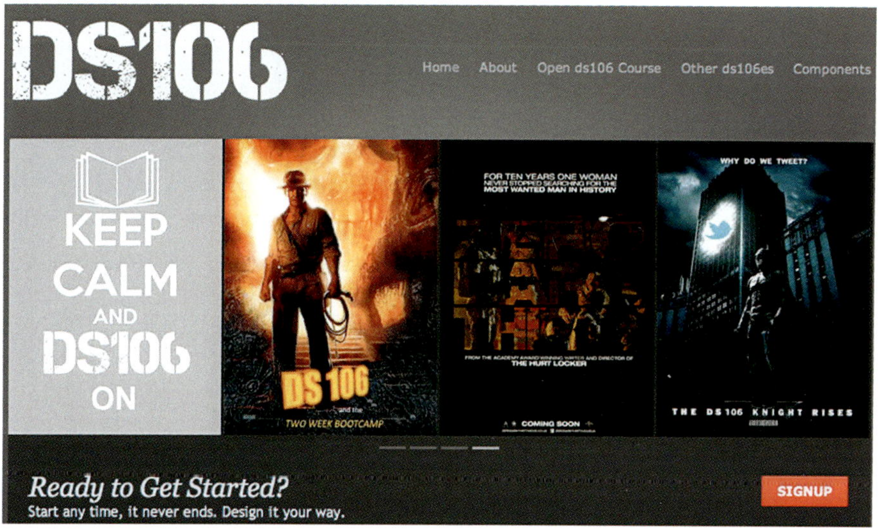

The digital storytelling MOOC (http://ds106.us/about/) follows the principles of the first connectivist MOOCs, and is a prime example of a cMOOC. The course is focused upon "questioning" the process of digital storytelling, encouraging learners to reflect upon the process of storytelling in the digital medium, through the analysis and discussion of existing resources, and through creating their own examples.

The MOOC is unstructured. Learners are free to carry out whatever assignments they wish to; they create, and analyze digital content, and discuss it with other students through online forums. Each individual creates their own web sites and shares resources that interest them through it, and the core of the course is focused upon the discussion and debate between students, when considering these resources. The emphasis is upon sharing thoughts and ideas, rather than attainment. So the MOOC does not contain any videoed lectures or set assignments; rather, the learner may choose to create a video to share with others, and has the choice of what "assignments" they wish to undertake. Also, unlike many other MOOCs, there are no set dates when the course runs; instead learners are free to drop in and participate whenever it suits them to, and to remain a member of the course "community" for as long as they wish to.

In the spectrum of MOOC activity, it sits at the end of the spectrum that puts the emphasis upon the individual learner and their knowledge, connections and unique interaction with content, rather than the end of the spectrum that "gives" content to the student. It was inspired by some of the earliest MOOCs that follow constructivist principles.

When mapped against the Lytics framework, we see the following:

Learner background and intentions

- Learners who wish to be actively engaged in, and in control of, their own learning. Learners with an interest in experimental approaches to learning, and see the learning process as a valuable part of the MOOC, rather than the transmission and absorption of content.

Interactive learning environment (community, content, assessment, instruction)

- An environment which supports high levels of social interaction between learners, and does not actually provide any substantial content, so no pre-recorded video lectures.

Technology infrastructure

- A distributed infrastructure rather than a single "MOOC platform"; this MOOC uses a number of existing, free technical platforms, including social media tools and free Cloud-based services such as GoogleDocs, to host content and to support discussions.

Phonar, photography MOOC

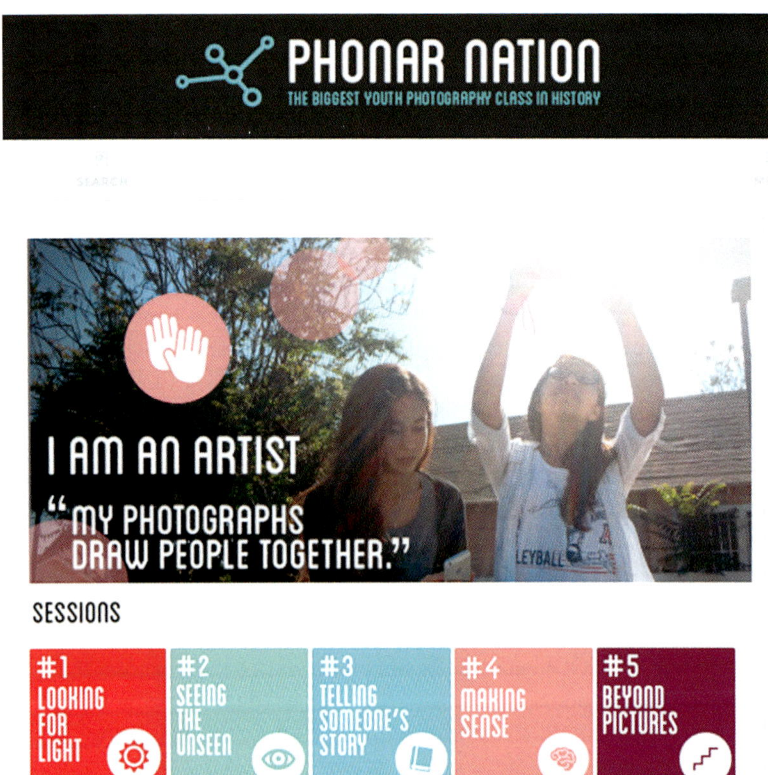

Phonar (http://phonar.covmedia.co.uk), a MOOC offered by staff at Coventry University in the UK, has been very successful indeed and has attracted over 33,000 students at one time since it was launched some years ago. It is unusual in many ways, in particular in how it was developed and how it is taught.

The course was not set up initially to "be" a MOOC, instead the objective was to offer the Photography course that is taught at the University of Coventry to a wider group of individuals than those who attend the course face-to-face, in order to bring together a much broader group of those who are passionate about photography and interested in building a career in photography or a related area of work. The intention was to help support students to achieve a greater understanding of what would be involved in this type of career and also the chance to develop their knowledge and, if possible, experience of the area, in order to improve the chance of them succeeding. So the course designer was particularly practical and sharply focused in what he set out to achieve. We will explore more about it below.

Learner background and intentions

- Brings together a group of students with a specific intention (to become a professional photographer) and strong motivation to study;
- Engages different groups of students with the same course—some attend the course face-to-face; some engage online; some meet and learn at local groups;
- Helping students to understand what is required for a professional career in photography;
- Connecting the students with professional photographers.

A student's perspective on Phonar can be read online (Daisy, 2013).

Interactive learning environment (community, content, assessment, instruction)

- Strong emphasis on social spaces and building up a connected community that continues to exist and live beyond the timescales of the formal "course";
- There is the concept of "mediated ownership" in the course, students are engaged with and own the course with the instructors, so they play a more active and constructive role than is usual;
- Also "opened up" to other experts to come and contribute (and critique).

Technical infrastructure

- Not using a specific platform, instead using a range of social media tools and "going where the students are already"—so Twitter, Facebook, Flickr, Vimeo, YouTube, etc. The choice of tools comes from the students and the tutor learns from them what they are using and why.

Understanding Dementia MOOC, University of Tasmania

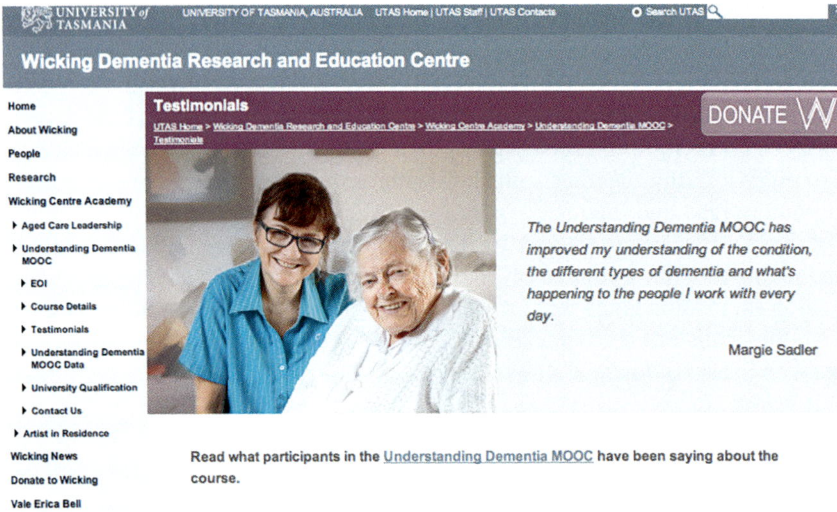

The Understanding Dementia MOOC (http://www.utas.edu.au/wicking/wca/mooc/course) was created because the University of Tasmania has established expertise in this area at its Wicking Dementia Research and Education Centre, and a strong reputation for the provision of postgraduate courses on dementia, and wanted to increase its international profile and potentially attract more students, some of whom might wish to study through distance-learning programs.

Learner background and intentions

- Group of students with a specific intention and strong motivation which has led to extremely high completion rates (over 40%);
- Cohort is made up of professionals who wish to study cutting-edge research in a specific area of health, and lay people with a strong interest in the subject;
- Both groups wish to acquire specific and up-to-date knowledge and to discuss issues related to that knowledge, as it is an emerging area where the research is constantly updated;
- Some students wish to progress to a formal program of study and achieve a qualification.

Interactive learning environment (community, content, assessment, instruction)

- Traditional model where content and instruction is provided by the institution;
- Strong community element has developed due to student engagement and motivation;
- A core framework of content supported by carefully designed learning activities.

Technical infrastructure

- Uses a single platform that is specially designed to support online learning activities ("Desire2Learn") rather than a new, MOOC platform.

Buddhism and Modern Psychology, Princeton University

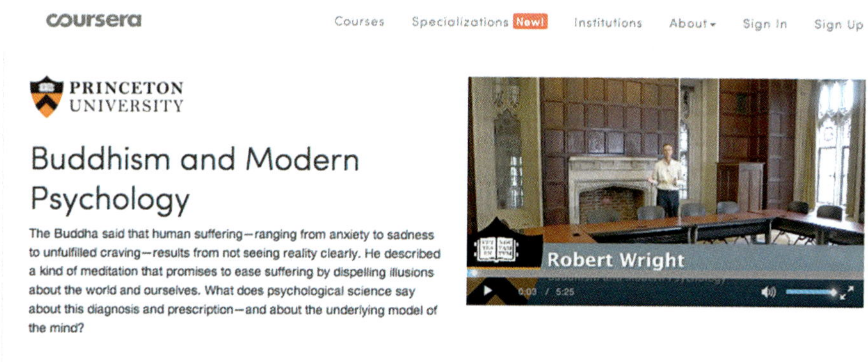

The Buddhism and Psychology MOOC (http://www.coursera.org/course/psychbuddhism) is the only example included in this chapter that is offered through one of the large MOOC platforms. It is included here in order to describe not only the xMOOC type of experience that is typically offered to MOOC students, but also that even one of the standard platforms can be used in a customized way by the teacher or instructor, according to how they wish to achieve the course objectives.

When the Buddhism and Psychology MOOC is mapped against the Lytics framework, we see the following:

Learner background and intentions

- Learners with a very wide range of background and prior knowledge, who are interested in learning about cutting-edge research and engaging with others. Some are practitioners, some are people with a lay interest, and others are casually interested in the subject area. It is unlikely that many are taking the MOOC in order to achieve professional development, yet the course achieved high levels of commitment and completion. The explanation for this is perhaps that the subject matter for the MOOC attracted a cohort with a particularly strong interest in, and commitment to, understanding the material. It is also the subject matter which brings together two areas of interest that are not usually considered together, and which are relatively controversial. The opportunity to engage with this kind of course online, where within a large group of experienced and knowledgeable others, was a unique opportunity to broaden and deepen knowledge that is directly relevant to life experience. A somewhat different area of focus than for some of the more technical MOOCs, it might be argued, but which nevertheless attracted particularly strong personal commitment from participants.

Interactive learning environment (community, content, assessment, instruction)

- The MOOC runs through the Coursera platform; video is played using HTML 5 or Flash, and the text displayed in the web browser and transcripts for lectures are available as text documents. Discussions between students take place in the Coursera discussion forum. There is also a separate Googlegroup for the MOOC.

The course is given a more interactive feel because the tutor creates informal "office hours" films each week in response to issues and questions that have been raised by the current students, giving a sense of immediacy.

Technology infrastructure

- The infrastructure is provided by Coursera.

Conclusion

We can see from even this small number of examples that there is a wide range of possibilities for how MOOCs are designed, and why different approaches should be considered, beyond the traditional, xMOOC approach of video lectures and automated assessments. MOOCs may be designed to meet the needs of a particular audience, because of the specific requirements of a particular set of learning outcomes (such as gaining professional skills) or because students wish for this approach to be taken.

So we see in the Phonar MOOC, for example, that the course was carefully designed in order to support the acquisition of professional skills, and to create a community of practitioners and would-be practitioners, who could support and learn from each other. This kind of approach might be applied usefully in many different domain areas, particularly where professional skills are needed. It may also open up interesting business models, as committed would-be practitioners may be willing to pay additional fees in order to gain special access to successful professionals, through Skype tutorials, for example.

It is also useful to note that although there are many advantages to working through MOOC platforms, not least the high levels of promotion that are achieved by marketing through a successful MOOC system, this is not necessarily the only or best way to offer MOOC to an audience; in fact, three of our four examples use other platforms which they either host themselves or through a third-party, or by using a combination of existing Cloud-based platforms. This reminds us that MOOC tools are at present not complex or unique as learning environments or for delivering content, and there are many other possibilities out there that are worth exploring.

By looking at just these four examples it becomes clear that MOOCs can be hugely varied in their objectives, structure, and approach to delivery. All of the example courses have been designed deliberately in order to meet learning objectives for the course, and because of other parameters, such as a commitment to using existing social media tools and software. The most important message is that they have been designed to meet the needs of their target audience, rather than driven by just trying to "deliver" specific content. So the design has been led by the perceived needs of users rather than being "supply-driven," and informed by deep understanding of the needs of the students for whom the course was created.

It is therefore important to carry out some level of market research and user needs analysis in order to be able to make choices about what type of MOOC approach to design. Clearly, in some cases, the choice of MOOC design will be limited by the affordances of the MOOC platform that is being used. In all cases, though, it is essential to gain a thorough understanding of the target audience of students and their preferences and priorities. The MOOC designers can then work within the limits of the MOOC platform to attempt to meet the requirements as closely as possible. This will increase both the number of students who sign up to take MOOC(s) and also improve completion rates.

It is also likely that, as MOOCs become increasingly common and online students become more knowledgeable about the potential of online learning, their tastes will become increasingly sophisticated, and they may choose between MOOCs based partly upon the design of the MOOC. Including innovative approaches, such as linking up the students with professionals in their chosen area of study, will raise the profile of the MOOC and attract more and better students.

In Chapter 16 we will discuss the issue of learner preferences, motivation, and learning design approaches in more detail.

References

Daisy. (2013). *MOOCs: A student's perspective*. topuniversities.com. Online at: http://www.topuniversities.com/blog/moocs-students-perspective.

Grover, S., Franz, P., Schneider, E., & Pea, R. (2013). *The MOOC as distributed intelligence: Dimensions of a framework & evaluation of MOOCs*. Stanford Graduate School of Education, Online at: http://lytics.stanford.edu/wordpress/wp-content/uploads/2013/04/Framework-for-Design-Evaluation-of-MOOCs-Grover-Franz-Schneider-Pea_final.pdf.

Further Reading

Levine, A. (2013). *ds106: Not a course, not like any MOOC*. Educause Review Online. Educause. Online at: http://www.educause.edu/ero/article/ds106-not-course-not-any-mooc.

Introduction to the case studies

4

The following six chapters describe, through case studies, a range of different approaches to Massive Open Online Courses (MOOCs) that are being taken by higher education institutions across the globe. There is a huge amount of MOOC activity underway at present and also new courses being launched every day. It is a volatile and fast-changing environment where innovative approaches to course design, delivery, business models, quality assurance, and marketing are being developed and tested out at a rapid rate. Institutional motivation is complex and the nature of the MOOC environment makes it difficult for senior managers to decide on the "right" approach to take.

We hope that this section will be useful for other institutions in reflecting upon their current approach to MOOCs or deciding whether to take a first step into MOOC creation—or indeed, to inform and perhaps reinforce their strategic decision that MOOCs are *not* for them at present.

Together, these chapters provide an overview of the breadth and depth of MOOC activity that is being undertaken. It does this from an organizational perspective, considering issues such as institutional motivation, governance structures, and learning experience.

Each of the following six chapters follows a similar structure. Each presents a fictional case study of a university that has developed an approach to MOOCs—either to offer MOOCs or, in one case, not to engage with MOOC provision at this point. The case studies are all fictional but draw together key learning points from real institutions. This approach was chosen in order to provide insight into real strategic decision making and current practice without compromising the anonymity of specific institutions.

It also gives us the opportunity to draw together some of the most interesting and informative practices to date. For example, some institutions have made a long-term and strategic commitment to innovation in learning and teaching. They are sometimes also taking a similar approach to their MOOC activity, so the experience of universities with similar attitudes have been distilled into a single case study.

The six case studies focus upon the strategic imperative, or motivation, which leads a university to engage with MOOCs or to decide not to engage at this point. We have focused upon the distinctive characteristics of that imperative to describe each case study. The six perspectives that we have included are given below:

- the confident entrepreneurs—those who are investing heavily in MOOCs and leading the way in shaping the MOOC scape;
- the old guard—those who have a long pedigree of investing in online and distance learning and are applying their experience to MOOCs, which lends competitive advantage but also may bring baggage and some limitations with it;

- the institutional innovators—those who are investing in MOOCs as part of a holistic strategy for institutional innovation;
- the opportunists—universities that have spotted the potential to use MOOCs to gain specific strategic advantage for their institution, without necessarily making long-term commitment to them;
- the cautious—those who are dipping their toe in the water but not willing to take risk or invest heavily;
- the old guard—the elite institutions that are circumspect about investment in any innovation, including MOOCs.

Our view is that these categories do not only reflect universities' attitudes toward MOOCs but much more broadly reflect some of the attitudes toward change and opportunity that are commonly seen in the higher education sector. We will return to this hypothesis, and its implications for strategic decision making in higher education, in the closing chapter of the book.

The confident entrepreneurs

5

The University of A is a research-intensive institution with a strong international research profile and high-quality undergraduate and postgraduate provision. It ranks in or near to the top 100 international universities in most of the world ranking systems. It has ambitions to be ranked higher still, to improve its research ranking, and also to improve the ratings for student experience for its undergraduate provision. In order to do this, it has prioritized focus upon the student experience through the development of a new student experience strategy, led by the Pro-Vice Chancellor for teaching and learning. It is currently in the process of implementing this strategy.

In terms of online and distance learning, the University has had a long-term commitment to using technology appropriately to support both local and remote learners. It has a history of investment in innovative projects and initiatives to support experimentation with learning technologies, and developed a culture of positive attitudes about learning technology that is visible at all levels in the institution.

The MOOC story so far

The University has made a substantial financial commitment to developing MOOCs and has led a high-profile and widely-disseminated MOOC program which it has communicated about openly through the media and gained a lot of positive coverage. It has also taken an "open" (though careful) approach to sharing its experiences and has produced regular, public updates about the methods that they have used and some of what they have learned so far. This has added to their status as a forerunner in MOOCs and international authority on the use of MOOCs in higher education.

The University is working with many partners and made the decision to work with more than one MOOC platform, so it is running MOOCs through two different external platforms.

At the heart of the University's MOOC investment program has been the putting of serious resources into creating a critical mass of MOOCs across a range of subject areas, levels of study, models of delivery and platforms. To date, it has run and delivered six MOOCs, and has already run some of them more than once, with new cohorts of learners. In order to dramatically ramp up its MOOC offerings, there are now a further 30 MOOCs under development. Most of these will be ready to be offered to the public within a year, giving the University a broad portfolio of MOOCs to offer.

Imperatives for investing in MOOCs

The main factor in the decision to invest in MOOCs was to enhance the University's reputation as an innovator in learning and teaching and by doing this, to better promote its already strong, high-quality brand. It has particular strengths in research and wants to be equally celebrated for its success in supporting learners and learning, and MOOCs provide an excellent way to market this element of its activity.

Related to this and of equal importance has been a drive to conduct educational research and development that will be used over the next 5–10 years to inform the way that the University uses educational technology across the whole range of its courses, and the way that it is able to engage with all types of learners—not just distance learners, but also what the University offers to on-campus students, to informal and lifelong learners, to alumni, and also to University staff.

The decision to engage with MOOCs has provided an opportunity to experiment in areas that are quite difficult to explore within the context of traditional university programs, because there are ethical issues with experimenting with pedagogy with mainstream students for whom accreditation is a priority. External validation by quality assurance bodies is important but can also stifle innovation. So this was a great opportunity to experiment at large scale and the University management perceives that this is where the most important return on investment will come from.

There are other secondary, imperatives for the large investment that the University is making in MOOCs. One benefit is the potential through MOOCs for focused and active collaboration with peer universities and peer organizations. Some of this will be with existing academic partners, as the University works with other prestigious institutions across the globe through various networks, partnerships, and informal arrangements. However, this is not just about institutions; the University is looking to MOOCs as a way to work practically with partners in other not-for-profit industries and the commercial sector.

Thirdly, MOOCs bring benefits as part of the University's outreach activities; they increase the ability to get the University's work out to a wider audience. More specifically, to engage with potential students who would not traditionally apply to any university, and to target global communities with which the University may not typically manage to build a relationship.

Context: strategic investment in online and distance learning

The University decided several years ago that it wished to invest seriously in online and distance learning and that it needed to carry out some action research in order to find out more about what shape this investment should best take. This was prompted in part by a growing awareness of the challenges for overseas students getting access to face-to-face courses, and an understanding that the maturity of key technologies, such as networking and content creation and delivery systems, meant that the large-scale use of online learning was now a realistic alternative to its campus-based equivalent.

For this reason, the University decided to make a serious commitment to online learning and set itself a target of developing and running at least one fully online post-graduate level course in each of its academic departments.

It set aside about £5 million (US$ 8.25 million) cash into this effort and also made available about the same value in staff effort (another £5 million or US$ 8.25 million). The program has been very successful and the University now runs a portfolio of almost 50 fully online courses.

This experience has been immensely valuable in helping the University to develop its portfolio of MOOCs; their experience has shown that building and delivering a MOOC is similar in many ways to developing and running a fee-paying, taught online course, and they have built on their prior knowledge, systems and processes in their MOOC program.

Governance and decision making

The initial decision to engage with MOOCs seriously was precipitated by an invitation from Coursera to join its platform. Although there was already an awareness of MOOCs at the University, and discussions had begun about whether, how, and when it might get involved, this approach sparked off a focused set of discussions which quickly led to a decision by the senior team to commit to a MOOC program and to join the Coursera partnership. This decision was validated by the senior team and then by the main strategy body for the University. The decision-making process moved quickly and took only days to complete.

Some other initiatives of this type would go through a slower, bottom-up discussion, and consultation process through the University Senate, but this project was like other similarly strategic and time-critical decisions and did not go through that process.

The decision making around the initial partnership with Coursera, and subsequently with a second MOOC platform, included focused activity on legal arrangements. A lot of specialist effort was put into negotiating the details of the contracts with each, and in particular to ensure that the University understood the exit strategy from the partnerships—where ownership of intellectual property for the MOOCs themselves was a main consideration.

The Vice Chancellor is personally very committed to the MOOC program and additional senior sponsorship comes from one of the senior management team. The program is led and managed from the chief information officer (CIO)'s office. Some new staff have been recruited to take on particular roles, others have been seconded into the team from various departments around the University. Other departments, including the learning technology and academic development teams, are responsible for the delivery of specific parts of the MOOC program.

There is also strong, distributed ownership of the creation and delivery of the MOOC program. Buy-in from the respective head of academic school for each MOOC is an essential part of the model. Every MOOC is owned by the School and not by the individual academic lead for that particular MOOC. Heads of School have been made aware of the level of commitment that is needed and their responsibilities, and the School has been given the right to veto involvement in the MOOC by them if resources are not available to support the MOOC, for example. Formal workload planning models are used by all schools and the MOOC work has been included in the forward planning of workloads for the key academic staff.

In the longer term, as a MOOC ceases to be a separate program and become "business as usual," this model will change and the MOOC program will gradually be absorbed into the existing University structures, and will be governed alongside other, relevant activities such as the other online and distance learning programs and local support for educational technology.

Resourcing

The total cost for MOOC development so far has been about £1 million (US$ 1.65 million) including all costs. The first MOOCs were more expensive to develop—the first six MOOCs cost about £300,000 to develop (US$ 500,000). Costs per MOOC are declining as the MOOC team gains experience and more MOOCs are developed.

Quality assurance

The MOOC program includes a strong emphasis on training and support for all staff who are involved in it. Formal training in how to support online learning has been put in place for the postgraduates who are doing the support. This has helped to achieve high and consistent levels of quality in the support provided.

The MOOC development model has been to create course teams with shared responsibility for the MOOC, made up of experts from across the University—academic content, technical, learning and teaching, quality assurance, marketing, and project management. Some participants have had to work with new people and new processes, for example, engaging with video production, scheduling, etc. They have had to work in a team and in a mutually supportive way. There has been a conscious focus on bringing everyone together to share ideas and this has led to a lot of creativity.

There are rigorous, centralized processes in place through the MOOC office to quality assure all materials that are developed. All materials must be checked by the office before they can be used. This means that the development processes and quality assurance are well understood by everyone and very rigorous. The academic leads on the MOOCs are happy with this approach because they do not want to be put in a vulnerable position by errors in the teaching materials, and they have been happy to adopt this method.

All MOOCs are reviewed before they are launched through internal peer review. However, formal testing of the MOOC materials "live" is not done before the launch of a new course as there is an understanding that MOOCs are always in a "beta state" (i.e., continuously under development). The approach is not to polish to perfection before materials are released. Instead, the MOOC team will make changes to materials "on the fly" during the course in response to feedback and commentary from students, in response to the focus of the discussion parts of the MOOC, which may reveal lack of understanding of the materials by a number of students, and by any problem with the materials that is observed. Materials and course design are subject to strong scrutiny, and they rely on their knowledge and experience to get this right.

Quality assurance for each of the courses sits outside the normal University course development process. It is generally the same as for other courses, which is to initially assure the quality of the course description and then to review the course as it runs and, on completion, to gather and analyze statistics and feedback from learners. It follows a typical approach, with some feedback gathered by surveying students and also tracking discussion and commentary that is made using social media. The quality assurance team looks at student retention and satisfaction values and uses these to reflect on the course design. These data are then brought together and presented to the MOOC quality assurance committee, to inform planning for re-running the MOOC and the next round of MOOCs to be offered.

Accreditation

The issue of accreditation has been discussed seriously within the University governance and it has been considered whether there are good reasons not to give credit at the present time. However, the current stance is that the University needs to gain experience and become confident in running MOOCs before they begin to offer accreditation. There are many complex issues related to accreditation which mean that it cannot be entered into lightly. Robust remote identity processes in particular would need to be put in place before accreditation by the University could go ahead.

Students taking the University's Coursera MOOCs will have access to accreditation through its experimental Signature Track service, so there will be a route to accreditation by Coursera, though not by the University. Participation in Signature Track will allow the University to gain some experience of accreditation issues—and in particular, whether there is an appetite for accreditation.

The University has experience of accreditation of online learning for its online masters' courses—these do not have a single exam so testing occurs through other processes. The key question for MOOC credit is about rigor. It is not really clear whether credit is really helpful to MOOC learners or not; the data indicate that they are not that interested in credit at this stage.

The University decided to run short MOOCs in order to get clear water between their traditional courses and MOOCs. They also know from research that part-time learners find it hard to sustain effort so short courses make more sense. Credit for short courses would only be small fraction of what would be needed for the award of a degree so they are not sure how useful it would be. That said, they have argued strongly that we should not presuppose why learners take MOOCs and what they want from them. The approach EU is taking is to offer as wide a range of possible outcomes as they can, and not judge what learners might need.

At present, the issue of University credit is hypothetical as all MOOCs are entry level only, and it would not be possible for a student to gather enough credit in order to quality for one of the University's degrees through only taking its MOOCs. So at present, the option of a fully online undergraduate degree is not available.

The University is observing with interest experiments at other universities which are offering formal credit for some of their MOOCs and will continue to review its position on credit as it gains further experience, and also as quality assurance bodies begin to articulate their position on MOOCs, as this is another potential barrier to fully online undergraduate degrees.

Partnerships

The University decided that there was value in engaging with two different MOOC platforms. They consider this to have been the right decision to make because of the value of learning gained from working with each of the different platforms, and also the opportunity to create more MOOCs, more quickly, and get them out to potential students.

That said there has been a big overhead to being involved with two different MOOC platforms. Each of the two organizations has different management styles and cultures and is different to work with, and this has presented some challenges to the University. They do not however regret entering into both partnerships and plan to continue their involvement for some time, at least.

The University is also considering possible other MOOC partnerships. It may potentially engage with another of the newer MOOC platforms that has been created, should the right opportunity arise, and it is also actively exploring opportunities to work with existing University partners to jointly deliver MOOCs. This might be at a large-scale or small-scale level, either a number of courses or potentially linking up in a specific subject area of mutual interest with a partner university. The ongoing review of its partnerships, and investing resources in strategically aligned new ventures, is a key part of its strategy for the future in many areas; MOOCs being an important priority but just one part of the bigger, strategic picture.

Future strategy

The University has made a long-term commitment to both online learning and MOOCs as one part of its online learning offer. It will actively experiment with many different MOOCs, in different subject areas, using different learning and teaching approaches, and working with different partners, in order to learn a great deal about how it should most effectively use MOOCs to achieve its strategy.

At present, the term MOOC is used to describe all sorts of courses, many of which are not massive or necessarily open, or may not be either in the future. The University wants to use MOOCs and online learning in a wider way than the typical large-scale

MOOC model; for example, to think about how to target MOOCs in schools, in Widening Participation in Africa, and in growth areas for student recruitment. MOOCs will only be used in a purposeful way and both with and through strategic partnerships. This is part of the normal strategic business of the University.

The University will explore and evaluate how to use MOOCs to support learning and move beyond the experimental phase and into the mainstream.

Thinking further ahead, and considering its long-term strategy, the current work with MOOCs and online learning could lead to more online-taught courses being offered by the University, and the practice for on-campus courses could become fully blended; for example, where undergraduates have to take at least one fully online module in order to graduate. The aim is to get ahead of their competitors by understanding more about online learning than them, more quickly, and being ready to invest strategically in online ventures in the future.

Key points

- This university benefits from having been the first to adopt MOOCs seriously and have received a lot of publicity from this public commitment so MOOCs have been an opportunity to further raise their international profile.
- This type of institution is most mature in its use of MOOCs and so has had time to reflect upon the potential MOOC partnerships and make informed choices about which they wish to engage with. Many of this group of institutions are involved in more than one partnership and/or also offering MOOCs on their local platform, as they have gained experience and confidence in their ability to not only create and offer the MOOCs but also to negotiate favorable terms with MOOC platforms. Their early experience has paid off and their successful delivery to date means that they may be perceived as "better" partners for some of the MOOC platforms.
- They are also learning about the potential to use online learning to support many different types of students, and for the recruitment of students, as well as to further develop their public engagement and widening participation missions.
- They are also in a good position to be learning about MOOCs from practical concrete experience, many have already run MOOCs at least once and some are running some of the same MOOCs for the second or third time. This gives them a lead in understanding more about MOOCs and online learning more generally.
- These universities will be able to build on this advantage to inform their local technology-enhanced learning strategy going forward, as well as their approach to open and distance learning. They have probably also gained a lot of experience in putting in starting and managing an intensive and high-profile IT project, again experience that will stand them in good stead for the future.

The old hands: experts in online and distance learning

6

The University of B is a medium-sized, teaching-focused university which offers a range of undergraduate and postgraduate courses. It is particularly strong in the delivery of vocational courses. It is one of the biggest national and international providers of online and distance learning (ODL). The University currently has about 2000 ODL students each year, which is about 10% of the University's overall teaching activity. The University has in place a strategy to increase these numbers to about 4000 students within the next 10 years, in areas where they have particular strengths, as they are seeing that traditional student numbers have been declining in recent years.

The University has built up its portfolio of ODL over the last 15 years. It started by developing several masters-level courses in areas where it has particular strengths in both research and teaching. Over time, it has put in place partnerships with other universities and colleges in a variety of overseas locations, and while the course content is all created by the University, the partners provide facilities and support to distance learners locally. It also franchises a limited number of courses to be delivered by other colleges and universities, some locally and others overseas.

The ODL portfolio now contains a number of programs at undergraduate and postgraduate level, and also some professional development courses that are offered jointly with partners. It also offers some of its programs in a more granular way, where students can study a particular module rather than a whole course. This is particularly relevant to some of the vocational programs, such as health care. The University also develops and runs bespoke ODL and blended learning courses for some of its corporate partners. These may vary in length from short courses, lasting anything from several days to several weeks, or spread over a number of blocks of time over a year, to a full degree course that runs over several years, part-time.

The MOOC story so far

The University has decided to invest in the creation of two MOOCs. The first MOOC will build upon the University's strong research and teaching profile in environmental studies. The subject area—flooding and climate change—has been selected in particular because of the recent public and media interest in these two subjects. Given the somewhat controversial nature of its focus, it is hoped that this topic will capture the public's imagination and encourage higher levels of engagement than the University might typically expect. The intention is for the MOOC to raise the research profile of the University in this particular area of research strength, and through this to increase its international visibility. The University plans to track, as far as it is able to (as not all data are easily available or can be mapped simply to MOOC students), whether this has an impact on either applications for traditional undergraduate, part-time, and short courses, including summer schools in environmental studies, and for postgraduate courses.

The second MOOC is intended as a "taster" course that will, it is hoped, improve recruitment to the online undergraduate degree in computer science. This MOOC will have two aspects to it: firstly, to equip nontraditional students with the study skills that they will need in order to undertake a degree online; and secondly, to equip the students with some of the basic, foundational knowledge that they will need in order to make a more informed choice about whether to apply for the degree program. The first set of skills and knowledge that can be acquired through the MOOC will be transferable to anyone who is seeking experience of higher education, and the intake to the MOOC will be open to all and not restricted to those who may choose to progress onto the online degree course. The MOOC will, however, provide an opportunity for the University to study recruitment rates for the online course closely and to monitor the conversion rate from the access pathway MOOC onto the online course—or to other interactions with the University, including a range of other courses that might be relevant to the subject matter of the MOOC.

Imperatives for investing in MOOCs

Particularly given its understanding of the online learning market, the University is very clear about why it is choosing to invest in MOOCs and the level of investment. The University has three main drivers for offering MOOCs. They are: to increase recruitment to the University's existing distance learning programs; to raise the profile of the University and increase brand awareness internationally; to attempt to achieve a position at the forefront of innovations in learning and teaching; and to be ahead of the competition in understanding how best to use online learning technologies to reach this goal.

Resourcing

The University has made a relatively small financial investment in the creation of MOOCs, as it has limited resources available for what it sees as speculative investments, so has chosen to only create two MOOCs at present. University management is divided on its perspective on MOOCS. Some see them as a serious threat to the University's existing portfolio of ODL courses, and believe that it should invest heavily in MOOCs in order to see off the competition. Others see MOOCs as having marginal educational value when compared to "proper" ODL, so do not perceive a major threat to come from those who provide them, and prioritize investment in new, income-generating ODL courses over investment in MOOCs. So the current strategy of limited investment and "waiting and seeing" is something of a compromise between these contradictory viewpoints.

Quality assurance

The University has in place an academic quality process for validating individual modules and short courses which was put in place some time ago because of the need to be able to quality assure its full range of programs. This quality assurance process will be used for the MOOCs also, as the University wants to treat the MOOCs with the same processes as for all its other programs. This is helping to achieve consistency of quality across its offerings.

Student experience

The student experience for ODL is well-constructed and highly tailored to the needs of open and distance learners. Through its years of experience of ODL, the University has learned that ODL learners have particular needs which have to be met in specific ways. So the University runs a dedicated support center that provides 24/7 help for all ODL students. It acts as a single point of contact for all queries, whether they are academic, administrative, or technical. The University has learned that this supportive environment is an important tool in helping students to cope with the challenges of studying alone, often in a time-pressured environment where they have many other responsibilities, and may also have financial concerns. Ultimately, the support center helps to prevent dropout and contributes significantly to student retention and student satisfaction with the program and the University.

The University does not plan to offer this level of dedicated support to the students on the MOOC. The support model for the MOOC will need to evolve over time, as the University learns more about the MOOC students, their motivation, and challenges. For the first two MOOCs, the student support model is based upon two mechanisms: practical support (for log-in queries, etc.) that will be provided by members of the ODL support team, but will be restricted to up to one full-time post for both MOOCs; and academic support, which will be provided through the online forums by a team of postgraduate students, under the supervision of the academic lead for each MOOC.

Accreditation

The MOOCs may function as both a separate module and a short course. There is a question that is still being debated about how the model will work for accreditation—whether to keep the MOOC completely open and charge for accreditation, or whether to get people to sign up from the start and pay at that point.

In the short term, the University will not offer credit for the two MOOCs, but will use them informally as an access route for further study, and use them as evidence of prior learning and commitment when reviewing applications for online and traditional programs.

In the longer term, there are options available that partly blur the distinction between the MOOC and the charged ODL courses. One of the interesting ways that the University is thinking about this is in terms of the entry point (admissions) as well as credit for the MOOC at the end of the course. There is potentially a route whereby the students pay for access to the MOOC and go through a limited level of assessment before they are able to join the course, rather than just thinking about accreditation at the end of the MOOC.

The University is debating whether it is useful to require proof of attainment as part of entry requirements, or whether to trust the applicant to make the choice about applying for a module. One of the challenging issues related to business models is that if proof of credentials is required, the costs of running the program immediately go up. So there are some complex and challenging issues to negotiate when considering how to make the MOOCs sustainable.

Partnerships

The University has a mix of many different partnerships in place. It offers dual awards with other educational institutions, mostly overseas, where part of the course is taught here and part in another country. It also has partnerships in place with about 20 corporate partners, ranging from large, multinational companies to small, local businesses. The corporate partnerships are mostly focused upon open and distance learning collaboration, delivered through a blended model where some of the course content and support are provided online and then the students come together for blocks of teaching and social interaction. The programs that are offered with corporate partners range from short, two-week focused courses on very specific topics, through to full degree programs that are developed specifically for that partner, working closely with them, and delivered through a combination of online tutorials, online content, two-day blocks of face-to-face teaching, and a summer school.

Relationships with some partners are developing, where they offer facilities and tutorial support; whilst the University provides the teaching, assessment, and accreditation. The University also runs franchised programs run entirely by partners, at undergraduate and postgraduate levels.

The MOOCs will be used to complement and supplement these existing partnerships and models. The University is having discussions with some of its partners about possibly offering a MOOC format taster course that would be offered to their staff. They are also discussing whether they might develop a MOOC together that would help one of their larger partners with recruitment of new staff; this model is one that is being tested out by some of the large MOOC platforms, and the University believes that there is potential to replicate it on a smaller scale, particularly for specialist areas of knowledge and skills where their corporate partner has difficulties with recruitment. There is potential to tap into a much larger market of possible future employees, and to use the MOOC to gain some prior knowledge of the aptitudes of those people.

Future strategy

The outcomes from the two MOOCs are closely reviewed and evaluated in order to understand the student experience, the costs involved, and most importantly, the transition routes to further study that have been taken by the students.

The learning from this evaluation will feed into the University's five-year strategy for ODL, which is under development at present. This will include a student support model that will bring together the range of face-to-face, blended learning, and open and distance learning opportunities into a single, student-centered framework. It will include targets for student numbers in open and distance learning at all levels, including short courses, but the emphasis will be upon offering the most flexible and adaptable experience to students, based upon rigorous costing. It will include an appropriate credit framework and emphasize engagement with, and delivery through, partners in the UK and around the world.

Key points

- The experience of this type of institution in ODL has meant that they have developed knowledge and experience of how to create online courses, what structures and expertise to put in place, how to support online students (who have distinct needs), etc.
- They have developed some understanding of the ODL market and how to operate within it, and their use of MOOCs will further help them to develop this understanding.
- They will have addressed issues such as quality assurance already; they will probably have well-established workflows for creating and testing online learning content which can be adapted for the MOOCs, and scalable systems in place, as well as experience of creating multidisciplinary teams for course development.
- MOOCs still present a challenge to this kind of institution. The business models for MOOCs are not clear and though they do not wish to risk ignoring MOOCs completely and potentially lose some of their credibility as an ODL provider, they can be challenging to the well-understood ODL market. How many MOOCs should they invest in, given the lack of financial return on investment (ROI)? What about accreditation if they offer it: will they risk competing with their own ODL courses? How will MOOCs affect their established brand as an ODL institution?
- So although they are in a strong position from many perspectives, these institutions are also in quite a precarious position as they have a lot to lose. They need to learn through experimentation and with a clear understanding of the value that they hope to create from some investment in MOOCs. Their main ROI may come from engaging learners who may then transfer to charged ODL courses in the future.

The institutional innovators

7

The University of C is taking a multipronged and holistic approach to the development of its MOOCs, and they form a key part of its overall investment in blended learning (BL) and online and distance learning (ODL).

It has taken a thoughtful approach to deciding where to invest in MOOCs, and its strategy has been to be both entrepreneurial, and take advantage of opportunities that have arisen through partnerships and new ventures, and also to plan MOOCs that align with its existing institutional strategies.

There are three parts to the multipronged approach. Firstly, the University has joined a regional consortium of institutions led by their national open and distance learning university. Through this partnership it is running three MOOCs in areas of particular research strength and where the University has been easily able to identify up-and-coming "academic stars." It has freed up these academic staff from their normal teaching commitments for one year in order for them to focus upon the development of the MOOCs and for them to provide an active role in supporting the MOOC students when the MOOCs are running. These MOOCs will run twice in the current academic year and last eight weeks.

Secondly, the University has selected one area of strong research and teaching expertise where it believes that it has an outstanding and specialist course to offer, but which at present recruits only low numbers of students, very few of whom are from overseas. The course is run at postgraduate level and focuses upon palliative care for cancer sufferers.

The MOOC content has been created by the University's specialist Cancer Research Institute, which has world-leading research programs into cancer treatment and care and which runs a range of face-to-face postgraduate courses aimed at both healthcare professionals and other specialists. This institute is providing support to students on the MOOC.

Students who complete the MOOC are eligible to transfer to the Cancer Research Institute's accredited postgraduate diploma in palliative care for cancer.

Discoverability of this MOOC is affected by not going through one of the major international platforms, and the University has had to work hard to promote the MOOC. It has used many of its existing partnerships, with specialist cancer bodies, to do this and the strategy has paid off.

The palliative care MOOC has run twice so far and will run again shortly. Each time that the MOOC has run, it recruited over 10,000 students and, notably, it has seen extremely good retention and completion rates; in fact it is outstanding when compared with norms for any of the MOOCs that are being offered from the range of different international universities. The University is also seeing good transfer rates from the MOOC into its postgraduate course. This is an interesting and useful experience for the University, which will inform its future approach to MOOCs, to its selection of new courses to create across its portfolio, and also inform its thinking about the "size and shape" of courses that it might offer—perhaps increasing its emphasis on short courses that encourage access to higher levels of study and also the value of being selective about the areas in which to try to develop a more extensive "market" for some of its quality programs that are not well known beyond a limited and mostly local community.

The third MOOC initiative where the University is investing is that after spending time on reflection and consultation, it has made the strategic decision to become a partner of the international, not-for-profit Open Education university (OERu). OERu has been in existence for several years and emerged from the Open Educational Resources movement, but has adapted and transformed in order to maximize the current interest in open, online, and free courses that the MOOC phenomenon has stimulated.

OERu includes as members a range of partners from across the world, with particular strengths in many of the world's leading universities with an interest in open and distance learning, and also not-for-profit foundations that have a philosophical commitment to open education. It has been an interesting decision for the University to join the OERu, as its profile is different from that of many of the current OERu partners. However, it has had a long-term strategic interest in, and commitment to, open education and considers that this meets with part of its mission as a public institution. For this reason, it has joined the partnership and is creating two MOOCs that are being run through the OERu platform.

One of the interesting characteristics of OERu is that it is not simply hosting open courses but is also offering credit for them. Those of the University's MOOCs that are run through OERu will be credit-bearing, so this partnership also provides an opportunity for the University to learn about the issues related to awarding credit for MOOCs and also whether these open courses attract a different audience than some of its other activities.

MOOC platforms

The University is unusual in the MOOC arena because it has decided to run some of its MOOCs, including the Palliative Care MOOC, from its own platform. The University has invested significant resources in the specification and development of the platform, not just in specifying and setting up the technical platform but also in developing the range of policies and strategies that are needed to launch a new, international venture in a way that is robust, secure, and legal. This includes the development of appropriate privacy statements, a branding strategy, terms of use for the platform, pedagogic guidelines to ensure consistency of approach and high-quality course creation, and technical and design guidelines for use by learning technologists who are supporting the MOOCs and MOOC content development. The MOOC platform is being developed jointly with a third-party supplier and the University team has worked closely with the supplier to get the platform design right and to pin down contracts and respective areas of responsibility, so that there is a minimum likelihood of performance issues when the MOOC is being used.

There are a number of reasons why the University has decided to take this approach. Most importantly, the team wishes to retain control over pedagogy and not be restricted in the way that they are able to offer MOOCs. Part of their motivation for MOOC development is to be able to experiment, and they believe that they will be much better able to do this in an environment where they have control over all aspects of the MOOC platform and associated processes. Coupled with this, the University wishes to bring the learning from the MOOC development back into the University throughout the MOOC lifecycle, and this will be easier to do if the MOOC is based upon the same platform that is being used for traditional courses, rather than a new and separate platform.

By participating in two other MOOC ventures, there is also the opportunity to learn about other MOOC platforms and to compare the pros and cons of each. This is a clear benefit, but comes with the cost of understanding each of the different platforms and being able to support the MOOC creators through the specific development and delivery processes. So it has added complexity and cost to the project.

Governance and decision making

The proposal to invest in the MOOCs was made with the support of members of the senior team and very quickly gained strategic support through the institution. This was largely because the MOOCs fit with strategies that are already either in place or under development at the present time and because the Chief Executive and other members of the senior team are kept well-briefed about innovations in the student experience, planned partnerships, and new strategies. The other factor that smoothed the way was that the senior sponsor was able to quickly locate funds that could be used to self-fund the initiative in the first instance. So a combination of political awareness, being prepared for new investments, experience of similar ventures, and good ongoing communication with colleagues, meant that achieving buy-in was an easy and pain-free task.

Not all necessary processes were in place, and the team that is leading the MOOC development has worked closely with the senior sponsor to create a new set of processes for the development of the MOOCs. This includes a two-stage process with an initial application and, on approval, the creation of a full business case for the MOOC to be developed and run. This is seen as crucial to the ongoing sustainability and viability of the MOOCs as a core part of the institution's teaching portfolio.

Resourcing

Even in an institution with a strong and long-term commitment to innovation in learning and teaching, there are still challenges when it comes to identifying funding for the development of new online learning courses. One of the main challenges that has emerged through the MOOC development process is due to the complexity of the resourcing arrangements. Unlike traditional courses, which are generally initiated, created, and run by a single School, the MOOCs involve teams of experts drawn from across the institution—and beyond. So it can be challenging to work out which department should resource which part of the MOOC development. This has proven to be a challenge and something of an impediment to development as it has slowed down the process of planning and creating the MOOC. Also, the MOOCs are being created much more quickly than traditional courses and using a nonstandard (and undocumented) workflow, so there is a lack of shared experience and agreement upon "who does what."

However, the experience of going through the development process now means that the University has put in place a set of procedures and guidelines that can be used for all MOOC development in the future. This has included some sensitive negotiation between central support departments and services and the academic Schools. Not all parties have been completely happy with the decisions that have been made but most importantly, and a good indicator of future success, is that all key parties have agreed to the plan for the way ahead.

That said, sustainable funding for MOOCs is still a big challenge to their ongoing viability and, until clear business models are created and well understood by all stakeholders, MOOCs will not be accepted as a core part of the institution's portfolio of activities. The evaluation of the current MOOC activities will be crucial in helping senior management to better understand costs and business models and hence to determine their future strategy.

Quality assurance

A comprehensive quality assurance (QA) process has been developed and put in place for the MOOCs. This includes four steps: the proposal of new MOOCs; QA monitoring as the MOOC is developed; testing and sign-off; evaluation and reporting.

Firstly, the MOOC team has created and put in place new, transparent processes for the proposal of new MOOCs. These processes follow two stages: an initial application process, which, if successful, is followed by the submission of a full business case. Given the early stage of maturity for MOOC business models, the business case may not contain balanced return-on-investment estimates but it includes a detailed analysis of target audience; an explanation of how the MOOC supports existing University strategies for learning and teaching, innovation, recruitment, or public engagement; description of the team that will create and support the MOOC; and detailed estimated costs for MOOC creation and delivery. This proposal is reviewed by the team that has been established for the purpose. It includes the senior sponsor (the Pro-Vice Chancellor for Education), Head of Quality, Head of Marketing, Head of e-Learning, and two Heads of Academic Schools.

Secondly, there is a process in place to monitor the quality of the MOOC as it is being developed. This includes processes for planning the content of the MOOC, according to agreed principles for learning design, and for monitoring guidelines for MOOC production, such as the length and quality of film clips. The process includes the external, third-party supplier of the learning management system as well as all the key members of the MOOC team.

Thirdly, there is a multistakeholder testing and sign-off process, which tests academic quality, instructional design, technical factors, and overall quality and accuracy. This step involves students, academic staff, pedagogy experts, and e-learning and marketing experts. The MOOC must satisfy agreed quality requirements before it is allowed to "go live."

Fourthly, and importantly, QA does not finish when the MOOC is launched—the MOOC is evaluated and reviewed throughout its delivery period through a combination of quantitative and qualitative measures. Data are collected from a number of formal and informal sources, including solicited feedback from students, through monitoring discussion forums and social interaction spaces, through the outcomes of the formal assessments that take place throughout the MOOC. These data are then pulled together and analyzed by the expert in-house e-learning team in order to produce a report that comments upon the experience of delivery of this instance of the MOOC and also draws out more general recommendations based upon this MOOC and others. This report is sent up to the senior MOOC steering committee and used to inform regular progress reports to the University's senior team.

This four-stage QA process may seem heavyweight but the experience to date has been that it has been a crucial part of the MOOC project, not only to ensure adequate quality in an external-facing, high-profile activity, but also to reassure colleagues that appropriate care is being taken in the creation and delivery of the MOOCs. The process also has created the "by-product" of emphasizing to all involved that the MOOC is a serious undertaking and one that requires proper commitment of resources in order to be done well. So the costs involved are deemed to be outweighed by the benefits.

Future strategy

The future strategy for MOOCs, and indeed for open and distance learning and BL, is subject to an ongoing process of planning, implementation, and review. The current published strategies for these areas will be updated when the current MOOC activity has been evaluated, within the context of other ODL work.

As described above, the current crop of MOOC developments are subject to thorough and rigorous evaluation and reporting, and this learning will be reviewed by the senior institutional team in order to determine their next steps of investment in MOOCs. The multipronged approach enables them to test out, and learn from a range of different MOOC designs, partnerships, platforms, and business models. This will enable them to make informed decisions about the future.

Key points

- This type of university has taken a holistic and long-term approach to innovation. Its leadership has put in place a strategy to support innovation through the whole organization.
- There is long-term commitment to improvement and adaptation at all levels of the organization, using a range of top-down and bottom-up interventions.
- This approach is not specific to MOOCs, but because the university is always reviewing its strategy and making incremental changes, it is in a better position than many to take a strategic approach to new trends as they arise.
- MOOCs have been undertaken as a highly strategic activity and are one part of an overall strategy for innovation in learning and teaching. They also feed into strategies for developing the institutional brand profile locally, nationally, and internationally, and public engagement in areas of research excellence. They also support strategies for recruitment and engagement of students.
- Investment in quality processes and procedures has been recognized as important from the start and due attention was given to these early on rather than retro-fitted as an afterthought. This includes a long-standing commitment to continuous improvement of the student learning experience, a commitment to BL, and using a range of different approaches to student engagement, support, and teaching.

The opportunists

8

The University of D is a research-intensive institution with a strong international research profile and high-quality undergraduate and postgraduate provision. The University is one of the few in the country to establish an overseas campus some years ago, and this now runs successfully, with a range of undergraduate programs offered to students living and studying in a Middle Eastern country.

There has for some time been a strategic imperative to increase the sense of the University as a single institution, in particular to bring the different groups of undergraduates into more regular contact with each other, to enhance the sense of the University providing an authentic cultural experience to its overseas students.

Previously, the University has investigated opportunities to offer undergraduate modules across the different geographic campuses, but found that time-zone differences and also the differing term dates made this very difficult to put in place. However, their recent experience with online education made experts in the University think about the potential of offering an online learning experience that could be opened up to all students, and also to University staff, who are based in all the locations where the University delivers its courses.

So these two factors came together in the development of what now might be described as a particular type of MOOC, a Small, Private Online Course (SPOC), but which at the time was seen as an experimental institution-specific venture.

This online course drew upon materials that had been created under the previous, externally funded program and supplemented them with other openly licensed materials that had been produced by other organizations. The materials were combined into a course sequence, and most importantly, were given structure and coherence by a set of interactive online activities, typical to a MOOC – a combination of asynchronous and synchronous discussion opportunities and online assessments. It was hosted on the University's own learning management system, which was considered to be robust and reliable enough to support the likely level of usage, and also importantly had in place appropriate mechanisms to manage user accounts and permissions to access materials that were needed for an internal, private course.

This early SPOC was very well received by students and staff alike and nearly 1000 individuals signed up to participate when it was first run, and several hundred more when it was rerun only a few months later. This experimentation meant that the University was in a place of experience and familiarity with some of the main issues related to course subject selection, design, platform choice, and implementation, when the MOOC bubble appeared on its strategic planning horizon in 2012.

Imperatives for investing in MOOCs

The imperatives for investing in the creation and delivery of MOOCs have been largely driven by the University's commitment to its ethical agendas. It has had a long-standing commitment to the open transmission of knowledge wherever this is viable, as exemplified by its commitment to open education. This relates closely to the University's mission to encourage participation and engagement with the University by as broad a group of students as possible. The MOOC movement was considered by the Vice Chancellor and senior team as a way to further reinforce these two missions, and to also demonstrate in a public, international forum their expertise and experience in open, online learning.

A secondary but nonetheless important imperative is to use the MOOC as a way to engage greater numbers of teaching staff in online learning, many of whom have no real experience of either teaching online or participating as an online learner. The University wishes to upskill its teaching staff so that there is a base level of understanding of online learning and its use to support a high-quality student experience, and the MOOC is considered as an effective way to help achieve this.

MOOC activities to date

The interest in MOOCs by the University's Vice Chancellor and members of the senior team has exerted a high level of pressure for the University to respond quickly and in the 'right' way to the MOOC opportunity. The local team of experts has been able to build upon their experience of a MOOC-like activity to quickly plan and create their first MOOCs. Yet even despite the high level of preparedness that was in place, it has been a challenge to meet the fast speed required to put in place a potentially large-scale, open, and externally facing MOOC of sufficient robustness and quality. Many new processes needed to be developed in order to ensure that the MOOC course had the right content, structure, and academic support for the externally facing course.

The infrastructure and systems also were reviewed before going ahead. Given the potentially huge number of students that might be recruited to a fully open MOOC, and the risks associated with opening up the local learning management system to an unknown group of users, it was not considered viable to use the local systems to host the MOOC.

Fortunately, parallel, political discussions had begun when the University was approached by several of the MOOC platforms and invited to become partners in their respective ventures. Evidence shows that students often move to a second or subsequent MOOC that is offered by the same platform, even though it is provided by a different institution, and Coursera currently provides access to many millions of current students with a much broader geographic spread than some of the other platforms. After long discussion and debate, the University made the decision to join Coursera based upon the established and well-tested nature of the platform and the large community of Coursera students that had already been recruited.

To date, the University has developed two MOOCs that are hosted by Coursera and are in the process of choosing which subjects to focus upon for a further two MOOCs. It is considering whether to also join another platform but it has not yet made a final decision about this.

Governance and decision making

The decision to engage was taken by the Vice Chancellor and then delegated to the Pro-Vice Chancellor for Teaching and Learning to lead a high-priority project to select the right partner to work with, and to oversee the development of the MOOCs. The MOOC project has been discussed regularly at the VC's weekly senior team meetings, and the senior team supported the decision to go ahead.

The other decision-making and consultation bodies of the University, Senate, and the Board of Governors were not involved in making the decision, but they have been kept informed and are supportive. This is an unusual situation but one that is not unknown, particularly for time-critical strategic projects such as important new partnerships or commercial ventures.

The MOOC development has gone through a much faster development lifecycle than most initiatives at the University, being completed over about 8 months from first idea to having first course ready. This is much quicker than usual, perhaps by about an year. Overall during the MOOC project, all decision making has been much quicker than usual because the mandate to engage with MOOCs has come from the very top of the institution. This has meant that resources were found quickly to support the MOOC project, rather than there being a need to engage in standard processes to make a case for the work and to bid for internal funds. It will be useful to evaluate this particular approach to review whether there are more general lessons that can be learned about the University's ability to respond to important opportunities.

Resourcing

Costs to date are estimated at about £30,000 (US$50,400) per MOOC—though this varies quite considerably, depending upon a number of factors such as the amount of material that already exists in digital format, the copyright situation, and complexity of multimedia that is required. This cost does not include all the academic time that is used to support the delivery of the MOOC. Initial funds were found from unallocated central funding and allocated by an internal planning committee, following a bid from the Pro-Vice Chancellor for Teaching and Learning.

Funding for the development of at least two more MOOCs has been set aside and a process is underway currently to decide which courses to focus upon. There is likely to be a spread of subject areas and level of study, with emphasis upon MOOCs that prepare young people for studying at undergraduate level and areas of research strength.

Academic resources for the MOOC creation and support have come from the academic schools. A really positive approach has been taken by the leadership in the academic schools, with genuine commitment to the MOOC project. The model that has been adopted has been to develop teams within the schools to develop and work on each of the MOOC. In the team, there is one clear lead academic; in the current cases these are relatively junior but very talented academic staff, who have a strong interest in innovative teaching, and are on the 'teaching excellence' academic track. Crucially, the academic leads are supported by the faculty education directors and heads of school who have supported them personally and provided a lot of their own time into advising on the MOOC content, format, and support model.

Another useful resource that has been put in place is a peer support model between the two academic leads for the MOOCs, who have met regularly to discuss the approach that they are each taking to the development of 'their' MOOC. This had led to some creative approaches being taken and greatly improved the quality of the MOOCs and is seen as particularly valuable as it has encouraged transfer of approaches across academic areas, something that is hard to achieve in traditional teaching situations. The University will attempt to replicate this peering model with its future MOOCs.

Staffing for the technical development of the MOOC project is coming in the main from the e-learning team that is already in place. There is a lot of specialist expertise in place that has been developed over time due to the University's interest in learning technology and open education, and there are strong teams with expertise in video production that have been brought in to work intensively on preparing the MOOCs. The different individuals involved in the MOOC creation and development are already experienced and used to working together collaboratively on similar projects, and this has meant that they have been able to 'hit the ground running.'

Quality assurance

The University is taking quality assurance very seriously. It is building upon its previous experience of developing online materials to develop a new model for how MOOCs will be quality assured. This work is being led by the Pro-Vice Chancellor for Teaching and Learning.

Quality is being defined as having a range of parameters, that is to include academic quality as well as a range of quality measures that apply at a more technical and process level. The model is based upon and similar to the standard University module approval processes, and it is important that the processes are at least as rigorous and thorough as for traditional courses. There is recognition that the context for quality assurance is different for MOOCs than for traditional provision. The University is attracting a much wider audience than for traditional courses, and there will be much less direction interaction between the University and the MOOC students, so this will impact on the quality of the student experience.

In order to address this, the quality assurance model will include extra quality controls that are specific to mode of delivery that is being used, and in order to ensure that, extra measures relating to the technical environment are put in place. For example, there will be further controls put in place around production quality for both video and audio production. There are interesting quality issues to resolve for video in particular, which will need to be addressed in the guidelines. Many of the MOOCs created elsewhere have included very high-quality video, not dissimilar in production value to the quality of commercial broadcast video.

There may be questions to address, though, about the extent to which all the MOOC materials really need to be of this very high level of quality, particularly given the significant cost that is then incurred. However, balanced with an awareness of cost-benefit is a desire to provide consistently high standards, particularly for the first set of MOOCs that are being released, as there is a perception within the University senior management team that the MOOC will be subject to strong scrutiny, not only by MOOC students but also by the media and by competitors.

So there will be some interesting issues to resolve as the quality assurance model develops and is implemented, and some of these issues may only be finally resolved after the MOOCs have run at least once. It may be that the University will gradually find a sense of its own 'brand values' for the online courses, in the same way that they instinctively adopt particular branding and identity for publishing and marketing materials—as with print materials, there may be questions about the message that may be communicated about the values of the organization, if all course materials are too 'glossy.'

For this institution, prelaunch testing has been included as an important step in the quality assurance approach. Traditional students will be involved in testing of the MOOC materials before they are released and academic staff will also peer review the materials to assure the quality of the content. Final sign-off will be made by the senior steering group that is overseeing the MOOC project.

Implementing a formal testing process is a different approach from some other institutions who consider the MOOC to be adequately tested by 'live' students as part of the first time that the course runs, as happens with traditional courses. The advantage of the MOOC environment is that they are able to make quick improvements to the materials in response to issues that are raised by students, rather than carrying out testing before launching the MOOC. This fits comfortably with the ethos of 'agile development' that forms part of the culture of open online learning, though perhaps does not sit quite as comfortably with some of the corporate University values and processes. In fact, it challenges some of the standard practices that have been developed and refined over many years. Should online learning adopt all the same processes as for mainstream courses, thereby potentially missing out on some of the benefits afforded by being able to quickly create, test, and update course materials? Or should they be created using a parallel but specific set of processes —in which case, does this threaten to undermine the credibility of the traditionally slow, mainstream processes, and will members of the academic community be happy to still follow the slow course development track, when they have experienced a faster, more responsive approach—and one that seems to work at least as well? There will be major issues for the University to address as its MOOC project continues and becomes more mainstream.

Student experience

The University has run one MOOC successfully and is now rerunning it for a second time. The learning from the first scheduled running of the MOOC has been extremely valuable and has led to many and varied insights into student behavior and student expectations.

The first MOOC had a huge intake of students, with about 18,000 registered for the MOOC. About 50% of the students registered when the MOOC was first announced and publicized by Coursera, and the reminder registered in subsequent weeks, with a peak in volume of registrations in the final week before the MOOC began—which coincided with another round of promotion and publicity. Some students also registered once the MOOC had already started; the 'admissions processes' do not preclude people from joining the MOOC at any point.

Coursera is able to provide the University with fairly detailed data about how the MOOC materials have been used during the lifecycle of the course. This data has revealed some interesting and perhaps surprising facts about the way that the students on this particular course interacted with the materials and with each other.

The student engagement or retention rate followed a pattern that has emerged to date as fairly typical for all of the large-scale MOOCs. Of the 18,000 students who registered initially, only half actually logged in to the course materials when the MOOC started. It is extremely easy, and of course cost-free, to register for any number of MOOCs and there are no penalties incurred by someone who registers for an MOOC and never takes it. So it is perhaps reasonable to assume that quite a significant part of the population might casually register for an MOOC when it is first publicized, but then later make the decision not to actively participate.

In this case, then, the 'real' student cohort can be considered to have immediately reduced from 18,000 to about 9000. Statistics show that this number continued to drop over the coming weeks until about 10% of the original intake, about 1800 students, completed the whole course.

These statistics may seem stark and even discouraging, but the University does not perceive it in this way. One thousand eight hundred students is still a very significant population of people who have engaged with the University over a period of time and in a very active way. This number far outstrips the typical intake for even the most popular undergraduate program—in fact, it is five times as many students in a single intake as the most popular course would recruit in a whole year.

In addition, the University is open-minded to the nature of the engagement that a MOOC student has with the course. It considers that the MOOC model is in very early stages of development and is immature. At present, most MOOCs are being run as 6–8 week courses with several hours study per week, and an implicit expectation that a student will want to follow the course through from start to finish, working sequentially, and with a consistent level of interest in all the materials. However, in reality, this may not be the way that people want to work with MOOCs; they may be far more individualistic about their motivation for engaging with MOOCs and so take a far more personalized approach. MOOC learners may not, in the main, be motivated by needing to complete a whole course and receive the relevant accreditation or certification. If this is the case, why would they need to complete all the materials, unless they really want to? The University is trying to not restrict its understanding of what is happening in MOOCs by limiting its thinking to traditional expectations around student motivation and student behavior.

For this reason, it has already decided to offer some so-called ‘mini MOOCs’—MOOCs that have a more limited timespan, typically about 3 weeks of study, and a more limited level of time commitment, typically about 2h per week—to test out whether there is a cohort of students who would prefer this shorter, lighter-weight course—and to investigate whether this then impacts on completion and retention rates. The mini-MOOC has yet to run but the feeling so far is that this is an interesting format that offers a different set of opportunities for both student and teacher.

The data also reveals some patterns about how students interacted with each other in discussion. About 10% of the original intake population contributed to discussions about the course materials—probably though not definitely the same 10% that completed the course. The course team has reviewed the discussions that took place to look at the quality of discourse and were really pleased with the level of discussion. They believe that this was facilitated by the active approach to facilitating discussion that was taken by the course team, in particular the postgraduate students who were employed as a formal part of the course team.

There is a sense in which the combination of motivated students with a real interest in the course subject area, the right course materials, and, perhaps most importantly, the right approach to encouraging engagement with the course by supporting discussion has led to the formation of a new online community. The proof of this is that at the end of the course, the most active cohort of students has also migrated in large numbers from the MOOC platform and now continues to interact through a dedicated online discussion group that is run through a social media platform.

Accreditation

The University does not plan to offer accreditation for any of its MOOC courses. As with other universities, it does not want to confuse the issue of accreditation for fee-paying courses, which are a specific and very different offer to the student, with what is gained through informal, unaccredited courses. It is, however, exploring opportunities to work with existing partners who may offer accreditation instead.

Partnerships

At present, the University has no concrete plans to offer MOOCs jointly with partners or to become partners in another MOOC platform. However, there are ongoing discussions about opportunities for partnership around MOOCs and online learning and also with existing partners where there may be mutual benefit in exploring an online venture. There is no reason why they might not consider joining other partnerships in the future; any partnership will be different and offer a different set of benefits and opportunities.

Future strategy

A full strategy is still to emerge and will depend upon the learning from the current experience of running both private, closed courses (SPOCs) and the large-scale, fully open MOOCs. At this stage, the University is committed to running both types of course, as they see strategic benefits in each. Work is underway at present to plan the next phase of SPOC and MOOC development, and a range of different subject areas are being proposed for inclusion in each type of online environment.

The University has learned from experience to be careful about which courses to select for development. It plans to take a highly focused and strategic approach to the development of both SPOCs and MOOCs, focusing on topics that are either of key importance for the University's mission, such as sustainability, or building upon areas of real strength in the University's research portfolio. Allied to this is the recognition of where there are really talented and articulate researchers who are well suited to the MOOC medium—and an understanding that there are some academic staff who seem to be less suited to 'fronting' a MOOC, during this experimental phase at least.

Key points

- Universities may have a particular agenda for creating MOOCs that serve the needs of a particular audience, such as overseas students who study at remote campuses.
- MOOCs present a particular opportunity for these kinds of institutions, as they provide a way to offer a new learning experience for all their students, who are located on different campuses around the world. They may find it better to restrict their audience by offering a Small Private Online Course, rather than opening the MOOC up to everyone.
- There is potential to reuse the same course model and content to run more than one type of MOOC and to cross-fertilize ideas from each to the other, gradually developing a portfolio of different course types.
- Whether to host an SPOC or an MOOC needs to be carefully considered because of issues of robustness of the technical platform when used by unknown but potentially very large numbers of students and authentication and access systems.

The cautious experimenters

9

In this example, University senior management identified several imperatives for investing in MOOCs. Initially, there was interest in joining a new and exciting venture that would put the University alongside some of the elite institutions globally that were engaged in MOOC. One of the early motivations for getting involved in MOOCs was to not be 'left behind' other, more innovative peers. As more investigation was carried out and senior management reflected further, other agendas emerged to have become equally important, with the other main driver being to establish their position as an educational innovator through large-scale and well-informed experiments with learning technologies, and to bring that experience to bear upon their traditional undergraduate provision.

As the University has begun to select and develop its MOOCs, and has been involved in many detailed discussions with other MOOC partner organizations, their thinking has matured further and other imperatives and benefits to the MOOC experience have been identified. In particular, their interest in exploring with the development of MOOCs in a particular area might support undergraduate recruitment, both by increasing the profile of specific courses, and also allowing potential students to gain a far deeper understanding of the subject matter and learning experience that they would experience, should they come to study on a traditional course.

The imperative to recruit to MOOCs is not as crude as looking at absolute numbers as the University is already oversubscribed. However, it perceives that with its global audience, MOOC provision may enable it to increase the diversity of its intake and potentially to attract students from geographic areas where it is currently underrepresented.

In addition, the University sees a strong potential benefit for MOOCs to enable it to involve a greater diversity of people in the University and that this may help it to further succeed in its public engagement and widening participation mission, to which it makes a clear and ongoing commitment. It is aware, however, that less advantaged and minority populations are not always well represented in the typical MOOC learner population, so it is taking a realistic but optimistic approach. It sees that this opportunity to experiment with global scale online learning will enable it to find out more about how to fulfill this specific mission, to the benefit of both local populations and those further afield.

There is a more subtle potential benefit about learner intake; it is possible that taking an MOOC will better prepare the student for the course that she or he will apply. There are two potential benefits to this: firstly, the student may demonstrate their commitment to and interest in the subject area by showing that they have completed a relevant MOOC and secondly, the student may then be better prepared when they take up their University place. This latter benefit may help to address some of the challenges of underprepared students that are fairly common at many universities. The University is using the MOOC experiments as an opportunity to test out these two things.

There is also an interest in exploring whether MOOCs might be useful for raising the profile of particular strong areas of research and teaching and attracting higher levels of postgraduate applications—and also attracting a higher quality of application. It is recognized though that this is probably a niche market with a relatively small number of potential students, even when considering a global population, so financial returns are likely to be limited.

Finally, the University is clear that MOOCs may provide one way in which to market the University to potential students and those who guide their decision making when selecting which university to apply to—including teachers, parents, and grandparents. They are sanguine, however, about how successful this marketing will be, and as part of their evaluation and analysis of their MOOC investment, they will explore the extent to which MOOCs have brought this kind of return on investment, or whether there are other innovative approaches to marketing the University that might create more value.

Overall, the MOOC project is a "nice to have" venture and although important at this particular time, and deserving of a high level of strategic focus and input from senior management plus commitment of resources, it is not at this point perceived as essential to the organization's future strategy.

MOOC activities to date

When the University joined the FutureLearn partnership, it committed to developing three MOOCs spread across a range of subject areas. The spread of subject areas was a deliberate decision as the team wished to get experience of developing MOOCs for a range of disciplines—science, business, and humanities—in order to better understand the affordances and challenges that each may present. There was also a political imperative behind this, as it is important to the University that this is seen as a University-wide activity and not marginal, or restricted to a specific area. That said, the choice of specific topics for MOOCs was made according to a combination of strategy and opportunity—so one or more of the MOOCs was selected because where there were already experienced online teachers who were enthusiastic to lead a MOOC course, and they believed that it would enable the University to get a course up-and-running quickly and relatively simply. It has not always been as simple as they had hoped, due to the quality of the video materials that had already been created, and some copyright issues, but overall they believe that this approach was the most practical and has worked well for the initial phase. However, future choices about MOOCs will be based on more strategic imperatives that tie into specific aspects of the University's overall priorities and strategy, as discussed below.

Governance and decision making

The decision to invest in MOOCs was made personally by the Vice Chancellor, after discussion with external parties and consultation with some of the senior team. The senior sponsorship for the project was then quickly picked up by one of the Pro-Vice Chancellors (PVCs), who has put in place a lightweight and fast-moving Project Board to oversee the initial phases of putting in place the partnership with the MOOC platform provider, selecting the courses, and now providing senior sponsorship to the team that is leading the MOOC development. The two PVCs have almost daily contact with the MOOC team and have a very close level of involvement in the project as it develops. This is due to the high-profile and high-risk nature of the project and is not typical for online learning and learning technology initiatives and ventures.

The Project Board is a small and focused but powerful team whose membership includes the PVCs for Education and for Enterprise, the Head of Marketing, the Head of Finance, the Head of the School of Education, and the Head of E-learning, as well as a dedicated Project Manager who has been seconded from the University's Quality Office to work exclusively on the MOOC project.

To some extent, the MOOC project has sat outside normal decision-making processes, particularly during the early phases where it would usually have gone through more standard approval processes of the Education Committee or Senior Management Team.

There have been legal issues encountered, which have at times slowed down the development of the MOOCs and which raise questions about the risk attitude of the University when approaching the MOOC project. The University's legal team has had an important role in ensuring that the MOOCs are following legal guidelines; this has been particularly critical because of the open nature of MOOCs—anyone can access the materials at any time—and also because of the media interest in MOOCs. Both marketing and legal teams have encouraged a careful and cautious approach and recommended that all MOOC materials are vetted carefully for any potential copyright infringements.

This approach was supported by the senior MOOC team in theory but has proven to be a significant hurdle to the smooth and fast development process, particularly where some of the MOOC materials include video that is not openly licensed, and which may for example include materials that include branded items in shot. The legal team has advised that these videos are not suitable for inclusion in the MOOC, so some video has had to be refilmed or not included and the course plan altered accordingly.

The outcome from the high level of legal scrutiny has been that the video production plan has not been delivered on time and the quality of the materials included in the MOOC has suffered, as the MOOC team had to chase up so many copyright issues. This issue will need to be addressed in the future by the University, which will need to decide whether they take a less risk-averse approach to copyright, as they do with other learning technology activities, or whether they invest more resources in developing new video materials where copyright is assured.

Resourcing (including funding)

There is a recognition amongst the senior management of the University that the creation and provision of MOOCs is not a free or cheap activity. They have been able to identify resources from existing internal budgets that were not fully allocated to pay for the creation and support of these first three MOOCs. This strategic use of internal resource in order to pump prime this first MOOC activity was discussed and approved by the senior management team of the institution as an appropriate use of resources. As such, the business plan for the initial MOOCs is clear.

Beyond this initial investment, any further MOOC proposals will need a clear and well-articulated business case to be made for their investment. Individuals and some departments are in some cases showing interest in developing MOOCs, but they will need to make it completely clear how they are able to resource the creation and support of the MOOC before they are able to commit to this. Either individual or department will need to explain if they have the resource available for MOOCs, and if so, why there is this flexibility within their workload allocation and budgeting. Any further MOOCs will also need to be self-sustaining in the future. So overall, the University is cautious about encouraging individuals or departments to attempt to engage with MOOCs without properly understanding the costs and benefits. A centralized approach will be taken to approval for further MOOC developments.

The University estimates that each of the MOOCs has cost about £40,000 to develop, but this does not include the cost of academic time used in the creation of the MOOC materials, nor to support the MOOC when it is running; these costs are being born by the respective academic departments during this pilot phase. The first pilot was the most expensive to develop as the development team was still putting in place appropriate processes and learning as they went along about the more efficient and effective ways to create the MOOC. The creation of high-quality video has been particularly costly, and legal costs (including the legal input required to check contracts and to ensure appropriate copyright for all the MOOC materials) have made up a substantial proportion of the budget. It is anticipated that some of these costs would reduce as the team gained more familiarity with the MOOC model and processes that are needed to support it.

Quality assurance

The MOOCs that are created are subject to the same course approval processes that are followed by traditional courses. This is considered to be essential in order to be able to ensure that quality standards are as high for any course that is offered by the University and to offer equity of quality to all learners, whether they are fee-paying or not.

The quality of the student experience during the MOOC experience is also being taken very seriously and the University has put in place strong teams of postgraduate facilitators for the first of their MOOCs in order to ensure that the students have a well-supported and smooth experience.

Student experience

One of the main current strategic priorities for the University is to be recognized as providing a very high-quality student experience to its undergraduate students. It does not in any way intend for the MOOCs to dilute its focus upon excellent, full-time undergraduate provision that is mostly delivered face-to-face.

However, the University perceives that MOOCs provide an excellent opportunity to experiment with learning technologies and with very large numbers of learners. They believe that learning about delivering content to many thousands of learners will help substantially with their knowledge of the technology that is available, how it can work best to support the kind of pedagogy that interests them. They are hopeful that the work that they do to create the MOOCs will give them far greater insight into how particular technologies, such as video recording, lecture capture, and online assessment, can be used to support an excellent student experience. This learning will feed back into learning on-campus and enable the University to make practical, informed decisions about how to best use these technologies to achieve excellence for their traditional undergraduate population.

So the University sees that MOOCs will help them to make their use of learning technologies more focused and effective—but not necessarily more efficient. It is clear that the experimentation with MOOCs is about an effectiveness rather than an efficiency agenda. Moreover, it wants there to be a clear separation between the courses that are developed as MOOCs and their provision for fee-paying students. There should be no suggestion that MOOC learners are getting access to the same experience of the University as fee-paying, traditional undergraduates. They are clear that there is a great deal of additional value that is gained by traditional students, in particular the level of contact with teaching staff; feedback on their progress through personal responses to assessments; and access to the broader University experience of on-campus activities, clubs, societies, and academic support, including provision for placements with partner organizations, and career advice. The desire to retain a clear distinction between MOOC provision and traditional provision is a key factor in the stance that they are taking at present with regard to accreditation and will influence their choices in this area in the future.

Accreditation

The University will not award or offer any credit completion of the MOOCs. Students will, however, be able to purchase completion certificates through the FutureLearn scheme, but these will be FutureLearn rather than University awards.

This is an important strategic issue and has been discussed extensively in the University and also between the University and its peer FutureLearn partners. After discussion, it has been agreed that there will be no plans to award University credit for MOOCs in the short- or medium-term future. The main reason for this is that it would potentially blur the boundaries between the experience that a traditional, campus-based undergraduate receives and an MOOC learner.

The University will nevertheless be investigating offering credit for MOOCs when working in partnerships with other organizations; in these cases, credit would be offered by the partner organization rather than by the University. This is discussed further in the Partnerships section below.

Partnerships

Partnerships are an important part of the MOOC project for the University. This reflects the growing number of important and strategic partnerships that have been put in place in recent years. The University is taking an increasingly sophisticated and proactive approach to partnership with a range of different types of organizations.

Its main MOOC partnership at present is with FutureLearn. As noted above, it was one of the first universities to sign up to the FutureLearn initiative and has a close working relationship based on mutual trust and benefit. The relationship is not without some occasional challenges, as is to be expected with such a new and ambitious venture. Communication has at times not been entirely smooth, in particular during the intense decision-making phase, when many different individuals at the University needed to be involved in the detailed arrangements of the partnership agreement and also more recently when developing the MOOC course and ensuring that the FutureLearn guidelines are properly understood and adhered to. Overall, the University is happy with the way that the relationship with FutureLearn has developed and feels sufficiently involved in key decisions. It is acknowledged that this may change in the future as the University's priorities and strategic approach to MOOCs evolves and as FutureLearn develops its own business models and possibly invites a broader range of institutions to become partners in FutureLearn. There is an awareness that the FutureLearn business models will no doubt develop in the future, and it is possible that they may not align completely with how the University will want to sustain MOOCs, so there is an expectation of reviewing the relationship at some point in the future.

Since the University first committed to its MOOCs venture, it has explored the potential to work together on MOOC development and delivery with some of its existing partners. Discussions are still ongoing but the types of arrangements that are being considered include jointly developing an MOOC with a professional association that would accredit the MOOC as part of its Continuing Professional Development program; and a partnership with an NGO to create an MOOC for its outreach workers in sub-Saharan Africa.

There are also less direct ways in which the University is making the most of its existing corporate partnerships in the MOOC area. It has a close and well-established relationship with some of its partners, which have specialisms and, depending upon the type of organization, have developed their own community of consumers, members, and supporters. The University is exploring the success of working through these communities and networks to promote MOOCs that may be in subject areas that are relevant to them. This is a kind of "cross-selling" in one sense and provides an interesting model for getting more value from partnerships that are already in place, particularly where those partners have ready access to potential MOOC students—who of course may then go on to engage with the University in a number of different ways. Depending on the level of take up that results from this new approach, it will inform strategic decisions about the creation of particular types of MOOCs in the future, for example by prioritizing MOOCs that draw upon research and teaching strengths that are likely to interest particularly accessible communities.

This university and others of similar reputation are already working to some extent with private providers of online education. Companies such as Kaplan and Laureate and, more recently, newcomers such as Academic Partnerships are working with a number of reputable institutions to deliver courses together in specific subject areas. There have been further approaches from several of the online education companies to the University to invite them to engage. This is not being taken up at present but is another avenue for further exploration that will be considered in the context of the University's overall approach to online education.

Finally, the University is also able to consider working with other MOOC platforms and not just FutureLearn; it may possibly look at developing relationships with other platforms in the future, and also one-off ventures working with existing or new partners, where mutual benefit can be identified clearly.

Future strategy

The University has invested in its MOOC project as an experimental initiative that will, it is hoped, provide it with several different types of hands-on experience and also a substantial amount of objective data, all of which will be used to inform its future strategy and tactics for online learning in general, as well as MOOCs more specifically. As described above, the University has foreseen several different sets of potential benefits to engaging with MOOCs and is using the creation and delivery of its first and second phase of MOOCs in order to explore and test out some of its assumptions. The University will be monitoring application rates for relevant courses; it will be monitoring conversion rates for MOOC students who have taken up fee-paying courses (where it is possible to do so), and it will look at its more usual market research data in order to try to identify an "MOOC effect" upon its reputation and recognition.

It is also carefully monitoring the resource requirement for both creating and running MOOCs, across a range of subject areas, to build up as accurate a picture as possible of the real costs of MOOCs. This will inform future decision making about whether to invest in the current MOOCs on an ongoing basis, as clearly the costs incurred in providing an MOOC are not only the costs of development of content, but there is a recurring cost in providing support to learners, in updating materials, and also any associated services that are run (such as specialist assessment tools).

So it is too early for the University to assert what its future MOOC strategy will be, but the main flavor to any future plan is that it will be very clear about which subject areas and levels of study (including Continuing Professional Development and informal learning) would best serve the University's overall strategy and help it to meet its targets for recruitment, marketing, and outreach; and secondly, it will look carefully at the possible partners with whom the University may work in order to maximize the benefit of their investment in MOOCs. They will be open-minded about the types of partners that this would include. It may include other universities that would traditionally be considered as competitors, because in the MOOC arena, traditional rules do not always apply, and the benefits of collaboration may far outweigh the limits or costs.

The University will also keep closely informed about further developments and trends in the MOOC world over the coming period, in order to understand the ever-changing political MOOC landscape, and equip itself to make the best guess as to the MOOC winners and losers in the medium and long term.

The strategy for MOOCs will be firmly rooted in a broader strategy looking at online learning in an inclusive way, spanning blended learning for traditional students and all its distance learning ventures, open education, and charged for courses, as well as MOOCs.

The general expectation is that the University will commit to a long-term strategy to MOOCs and that there will be a range of different types of MOOCs developed, with a range of subject areas, level of study, partners, and business models. Whatever approach it decides to take, there is no doubt that it will be considered at the highest level of the institution and will form a core part of future strategy.

Key points

- Some high-quality and research-intensive institutions are experimenting with MOOCs in a cautious way.
- Their traditional approach to online learning has been to invest in excellence and high-quality support, but to allow change to come from the bottom up rather than supporting it from the top downwards.
- Their interest in MOOCs is driven largely by not wanting to be left behind new approaches that are being explored by their peer group. There is a political element of wanting to be seen to join "the right club" and be associated with other similar, high-quality organizations, in order to further extend and deepen their brand and identity.
- They are investing fairly substantially in MOOCs and are interested to see what value they can bring to the institution's strategic objectives, but MOOCs are not seen as critical to their future performance, nor necessarily a major area of investment.
- For these institutions more than for any other group, MOOCs are seen as a way to promote the reputation and brand of the university.

The old guard

10

The University of F is a prestigious institution with a long history and pedigree. It is ranked as one of the top four institutions in its home country and one of the top universities in the world, appearing in the top 25 universities in the Times Higher Education World Reputation Rankings. It has a very strong reputation for research and receives 70% of its income from research funding, but also has a high reputation for the quality of its teaching, and it is one of the most heavily subscribed institutions in the country with an average of five applications for every place.

The University prides itself upon its low staff to student ratios and small-group teaching approaches; it generally scores highly in national surveys of student experience, although there is some difference in ratings between subject disciplines. Its recent focus has been to strengthen its reputation for excellent education still further, and to ensure consistency of quality across all courses.

Historically, the University has taken a measured approach to engaging with learning technology. It has been an early adopter of some systems, mostly driven by innovative teachers who have experimented with new approaches because they want to support their learners better. Particular disciplines, such as medicine, have developed their own online learning systems because they fit the teaching approaches for that subject area. This type of innovation has mostly been "bottom up" and although supported and encouraged through central support, and awarded through University teaching quality recognition schemes, it has never been mandated.

About 10 years ago, the University put in place a Virtual Learning Environment or Learning Management System, and it mandates as part of its learning and teaching strategy that a level of course information should be provided for all undergraduate courses. However, this is often fairly limited and interaction with the online systems is in some cases managed by administrative departments rather than faculty, so that many faculty have a limited interaction with online learning systems, and potentially little or no understanding of the pedagogy of online learning.

Overall, the picture of blended learning for traditional undergraduate students is that there are pockets of innovative and ground-breaking practice, but the general level of adoption is low and unsophisticated, with little sharing of practice among colleagues and across disciplines. There is central support available to teaching staff, in terms of video production, multimedia, lecture capture, and online assessment systems, but this is made available on an optional basis and there is no consistent approach in place to the use of these technologies. In surveys, students have commented on the lack of take up and use of learning technologies and the low level of awareness and understanding of them by some of their teachers. At the same time, though, students value the close contact that they have with academic staff, small-group sizes for teaching, and access to wide ranges of resources.

The University has experimented with some limited distance and online learning ventures over the past 20 years or so, focused at postgraduate level, working in partnership with other prestigious institutions and commercial organizations, but these have been pilot activities that have never really taken off or gained a prominent place in the University's strategy. The overall approach has been conservative and care has been taken not to threaten or undermine the international brand of the institution.

Open education

In line with its mission to engage with the public through outreach activities, the University has engaged with the production and promotion of Open Educational Resources (OER) over the past 5–10 years. It successfully sought external funding to create some exemplar OER materials and these were well received, and acted as a focus of experimentation for specific groups of academic staff, working closely with learning technologists. The successful bids for external funding led to investment by the University in a local repository for OER, which has provided a focus for the ongoing creation of further open resources, supported by the learning technology department. There has been no compulsion for teaching staff to engage in this, or to deposit or share their materials as open resources or under a particular licensing framework. The repository has been promoted as part of various University schemes to recognize and celebrate innovation in teaching, but there has not been any specific incentive made available to encourage further creation of resources, or to reward those who make this a priority over some of their other commitments (research, publishing, and administration).

The University has also promoted its OER resources externally through national UK repositories such as Jorum, and commercial offerings such as iTunesU. There is an ongoing program of support to academic staff to create OER, but there is no current OER strategy in place. The Head of Learning Technology is a strong supporter of OER and is engaged with various national and international projects. Working with some of the more OER-aware academic leaders, he has drafted an OER strategy that has been reviewed and discussed by the Education Committee, but no decision has yet been made about the preferred approach to take. The advent of MOOCs has added complexity to the discussions.

MOOCs

The University Senior Management team has observed the development of MOOCs with an interested but cautious eye. There has been quite a high level of interest generated by the national and international press that has reached the attention of some members of the Board of Governors, who have raised MOOCs as an agenda item at one of their meetings. The Vice Chancellor has also taken a personal interest in the issue; MOOCs are of particular interest to her because of the caliber of the US institutions that have been taking the lead with MOOC development; these are peer organizations to the University so their significant investment in MOOCs is more relevant than for some other online ventures.

In parallel, the University has been approached by all main international MOOC players and by the UK MOOC platform, FutureLearn. It has had high-level meetings with some of the platforms and has pursued these discussions seriously but carefully, with a particular interest in understanding the contractual arrangements that would be put in place were the University to decide to partner with a particular platform, or platforms. The emphasis has been upon careful fact-finding in order to make an informed approach, but with an underlying sense that the University has no need to enter into this kind of venture unless it can see a very strong case to do so. As with any major strategic initiative with potential international visibility and impact, the governors and senior management consider that the risk to reputational loss through an ill-considered partnership far outweighs the disbenefit of being slow to engage, or not to engage at all. To date, the strategic decision has been not to engage with MOOCs, but to keep an open ear and mind, to pursue ongoing discussions with selected potential partners and dialogue with possible philanthropic investors.

Some private providers of online and distance learning have also managed to engage the University in dialogue about possible partnerships or mutually beneficial relationships. Engagement with private providers is also being considered but being treated with even greater caution than the University-led MOOC platforms. The benefits and terms of any engagement would need to be carefully appraised and accepted before any partnership might take shape, and this seems the least likely outcome of discussion.

The University is currently reviewing its position with regard to learning technology and plans to publish a new Technology Enhanced Learning (TEL) strategy within the next 12 months. Both MOOCs and OER will feature in this strategy. The University is currently fact-finding and engaging in debate with senior engagement and local experts in order to determine its position. Part of the drafting of the strategy to date has included consultation with the academic body about their views on learning technology, and there has been a strong positive engagement in this exercise, not least because academic staff are also sensitive to the recent publicity about MOOCs in the media and are keen to propose suggestions for the development of both OER and MOOCs. The student body is also interested and enthusiastic about activities that enhance the global reach and brand of the University, and surveys have shown that they are supportive of the current range of open ventures. Their attitude toward MOOCs that would be open freely to anyone has not yet been tested.

There is also discussion in the University about offering online materials to a more limited and select group, either alumni or the current staff and student body, or perhaps both. The Harvard move to offer Small Private Online Courses has generated interest and attention, and will also be considered as part of the new TEL strategy.

The University will wish to carefully harness the enthusiasm of both teachers and students and to build upon it, while carefully managing its outward-facing provision and brand. Quality assurance will be of paramount importance, starting from the selection of appropriate courses and the team who would create the course, and running through the set of processes that would be put in place to ensure appropriate quality of materials and support. Any decision to engage with MOOCs will be carefully handled and is likely to be very limited in the first instance, with perhaps one or two pilots. It is also likely that pilots would be hosted by a local platform rather than through partnership with an existing platform, due to the overriding desire to manage and protect the University brand.

Key points

- Some of the most elite global institutions are very cautious about engaging with online learning and MOOCs in particular.
- Their desire to maintain their brand and reputation is stronger than the drive to embrace change or the risk of being perceived as laggardly and out of date.
- They are highly sensitive to the attitudes of their main competitors and are influenced by the decisions that their peers make.
- Although they are not interested in joining large consortia, they are interested in partnerships, as long as they are "the right kind."
- These universities are very attractive to both private and public investors. We should expect to see some interesting partnerships emerge, as this new wave of investment in online education continues to develop.

Key issues that emerged from the case studies

11

This chapter draws out the main conclusions from the six case studies and provides a picture of the most significant decisions that universities are making about Massive Open Online Courses (MOOCs) and the approaches that they are taking to planning and implementing them.

Imperatives for engagement in MOOCs

There are a range of different reasons as to why institutions are engaging in MOOCs. As we see from the case studies, some universities have very specific agendas that they wish to pursue, for example, the **entrepreneurial** institutions, which are investing heavily in developing MOOCs as part of an explicit strategic agenda: to establish themselves as key innovators in learning technology and also to enhance their international brand.

For others, particularly those with a strategic commitment to **online and distance learning**, MOOCs are potentially a major threat and these organizations are investing actively in a strategy that builds upon their existing expertise. They are selectively investing in MOOCs that help showcase their strengths and highlight their existing portfolio, and treading a careful line between using MOOCs to market themselves without undercutting their current business models and income streams. These institutions are potentially in a high-risk game: MOOCs have the potential to seriously disrupt their business over relatively short timescales, in a way that they do not for more traditional institutions.

For other institutions, in particular the **cautious experimenters**, the engagement with an MOOC platform may be based upon a desire to maintain their position in a competitive market, so although they do wish to invest in innovation in learning, their approach owes more to "keeping up with the competition" than trying to lead the way. For these institutions, working with MOOC platforms seems to provide a lower risk way to engage with MOOCs, without having to invest heavily in infrastructure, systems, or processes.

There is another strong motivating factor: to examine actively some of the promises that have been made about the benefits of MOOCs to universities. These institutions are also interested in testing out whether MOOCs may lead to higher application rates for some courses, may develop international markets, and may also encourage local academic staff to try out learning technologies with local students.

In some cases, this range of possible benefits are all being explored through just one or two small-scale MOOC experiments. For these institutions, it may be challenging to understand in any depth whether their MOOCs have brought these benefits or not, given the number of different factors at play, the limited timescales, and the small number of experiments carried out. They will no doubt be watching their colleagues and competitors closely before they make decisions about whether to continue to run MOOCs, to increase or cease investment.

This speaks to the more general agenda about innovation in higher education. As we have noted earlier, faced by challenge and opportunity, the higher education system is in need of reform and investment decisions need to be made carefully and well. However, a consistently conservative approach to investing in change ("do nothing and hope for the best") does not make strategic sense. For some, the problem stems from lack of clear strategy for the future upon which to base decisions—whether they are about investing in MOOCs, another significant new venture, or making other disruptive decisions, such as refocusing or ceasing research efforts, new partnerships, or growth. In the MOOC area, as for many others, the key point is for the institution to understand what it plans to achieve through the investment, to commit to putting in place adequate resources, systems, and processes plus senior management sponsorship, in order to really test out the possibilities, and to be clear about how they evaluate the success of the venture. Without this, they risk missing out on an opportunity to make the right strategic decision about their future strategy for online learning.

Governance and decision making

The most striking aspect of MOOC development has been the speed at which universities and colleges have committed reputation and resources to them. When we consider the governance and decision making that has gone on behind the scenes in order to make this possible, the reason behind this becomes clear. In all the case studies that we describe, the mandate to "do MOOCs" has come from the senior management of the institution, many cases, specifically by the Vice Chancellor (or equivalent). In other cases, the drive has come from the senior management team, championed by one or two members of the team who are working at a very senior level within the organization.

There are helpful and unhelpful aspects to this level of senior sponsorship to the MOOC project. It is mostly positive, as it means that decisions are made much faster than usual and potential barriers that may usually crop up, either through formal decision-making routes or a lack of impetus for investment in change, are easily removed or circumvented. The less positive side is that it can at times lead to a situation where the MOOC project has not been properly embedded into institutional processes and procedures, such as quality assurance, and these processes need to be retrofitted after the fact, rather than before. There can also be a lot of pressure on stretched resources to "get the MOOC out there" which can be challenging for staff if they have been entering into new partnerships and dealing with sensitive issues such as copyright and academic ownership for digital resources.

Overall, though, senior sponsorship is positive for the MOOC project and also for related institutional strategies. In many cases, it has raised the profile of online learning much more broadly, and will lead to more comprehensive and longer term debates about institutional strategy in this area.

This includes developing the institutional approach to online learning (including the local strategy for blended learning) with the engagement and support of senior decision-makers, an approach that will lead to more focused use of resources, more support for change, and, ultimately, a better student experience.

Quality assurance

There are three approaches to quality assurance (QA) described in the case studies. The first is to use the QA processes that are already in place in the university. This has the advantage of giving similar importance to QA for MOOCs as for traditional courses, and should be quick and easy to put in place. The disadvantage may be that the current QA processes are based upon a slow life cycle for the development of new courses, and this can restrict the speed at which MOOCs can be made available.

The second approach is to circumvent the usual QA processes and put in place lightweight processes, where the sponsorship group for the MOOC project makes decisions about when the MOOC is ready to "go live." This model works well in terms of speed and is probably acceptable for developing just one or two MOOCs, where the institution is under pressure to complete and launch the MOOC, but has risks attached to it as the QA may be fragmented and there is a risk that all the key aspects of the MOOC may not be scrutinized as carefully as they need to be. It can, however, be difficult to move from this model to either the first or third approach, particularly if the institution has not yet decided to commit strategically to MOOCs.

The third approach is to develop new, thorough QA processes specifically for the MOOC project or program. Some of these processes may be based upon existing QA arrangements, particularly where these already exist for online programs, but they will have been adapted so that they work particularly well for the MOOC model. The **institutional innovators** case study provides a good example of this approach. It is the most in-depth and thorough model, and is also the most expensive and complex to implement, and may feel like overkill for a university that has not yet decided whether to commit to MOOCs in the medium or long term.

Partnerships and MOOC models

Partnerships are emerging as a key factor for a growing number of MOOCs. These may be partnerships with other institutions, with charities and other not-for-profit organizations, or with commercial organizations. Universities are actively seeking ways to work with their existing partners to develop MOOCs together, for example, working with another academic institution through a global consortium. They are also working with professional associations to develop MOOCs jointly, and putting in place creative approaches to course design and accreditation that build upon the respective expertise of each partner.

This is in addition to the key partnerships that underpin membership of the MOOC platforms, where universities and the MOOC platforms are working together under the terms of specific legal and financial arrangements. These partnerships are also part of the MOOC experiment and part of the overall learning experience, and will no doubt lead to a range of different approaches being explored in the future.

Costs and business models

The costs of developing and business models for sustaining MOOCs are the key factors in the decision to invest in development and require more detailed analysis, and are each discussed in detail in Chapters 13 and 14.

We will also use the experience of the case studies, and accepted good practice for the management of projects and programs, to set out, in the next chapter, a summary of the main steps involved in MOOC development.

Planning the MOOC project

12

Introduction

This chapter draws upon the experience gained by those institutions that contributed to the case studies and provides guidance on the main steps involved in devising and implementing a MOOC strategy. It draws upon established good practice for program and project management, using the terminology that is common to the PRINCE2 and Managing Successful Programmes (MSP) methodologies. It may be argued that a large-scale MOOC development is better viewed as a program made up of a number of separate projects and other activities, rather than as project; in this case, the MSP methodology may be of greater value. For the sake of simplicity we refer to the MOOC "project" rather than the MOOC "program" through this book; this should be read as shorthand for either project or program, depending upon the local context.

Following this chapter, separate chapters provide more detailed analysis of two crucial aspects of the MOOC planning: costings and business models. The following three chapters then look at three areas that should inform the future MOOC strategy development: understanding the market—the learner as consumer, data and analytics, and the developing MOOC market.

Based on the experience of the university case studies, this section briefly describes a recommended set of processes to follow in setting up the MOOC project or program. These are suggestions and not a proscribed methodology; each institution will need to design the process that fits their local situation, constraints and existing strategies, as well as projects and initiatives.

For simplicity, this is described as a linear process. The reality will be a series of recurring processes in some cases, in particular for stakeholder engagement, evaluation, and quality assurance. It is recommended that the MOOC management team maps out the processes and relationships between them as part of the overall planning process.

Stage 1: initial planning (project initiation)

There are four significant steps that need to be undertaken during the initial planning or project initiation process. These are to review the landscape for the MOOC development, to plan alignment with other strategies, to conduct market research, and to explore partnerships and competitors.

- **Review the landscape: strategies and activities**
  MOOC development cannot take place within a vacuum of organizational strategies, plans, and activities. As part of the initial planning process, you should review the organizational landscape and identify those existing strategies, plans, and activities that are most relevant. This will depend upon your organizational context but is likely to include the university strategy, for guidance on institutional priorities, such as internationalization, student engagement, and expansion; the learning and teaching strategy (which may or may not include a technology-enhanced learning strategy); and the open and distance learning strategy, where this exists.
  You will also want to ensure that you have a clear and up-to-date picture of the current learning technology landscape within the institution, to understand where expertise lies, where activities are already taking place, and who the institutional leaders and influencers are in this area. This may include expertise in university management structures, academic departments, technology or educational departments or services, and library services. If you have time, it is useful to try to build up a local picture of significant information technology (IT) initiatives that are current or have run recently, and try to get a sense from key informants (perhaps through interviews or informal conversations) of what has worked well and what has not. This is a very useful exercise that can help you to avoid some of the more obvious pitfalls, and also to begin to build up a sense of key stakeholders.
- **Plan alignment with other strategies**
  The next step is to plan how the MOOC project will align with the existing strategies. This activity will help you to make the case for the MOOC project, by making it clear how the MOOC is helping the delivery of that strategy, for example, by providing an opportunity for the university to develop its international marketing. It will also help you to identify ownership for the most relevant existing activities and resources, including the key stakeholders with whom you will need to engage in order to develop your MOOC plan. For example, which of the Pro-Vice Chancellors, Deans, or other stakeholders (e.g., Head of Marketing) you will need to include in the initial planning process.
- **Market research**
  This is an essential step and one that is discussed in more detail in the next chapter, when we consider resourcing for the project. Some of the criticism of MOOCs (and online learning more generally) is that they may sometimes be a "solution looking for a problem" rather than being led by the needs of users. MOOC development is not a cheap activity and is likely to be costly in terms of risk and human capital, as well as financial investment. It is crucial that you and your team have done as much as you can to identify your target group of potential students before you start planning, and to prioritize the subject areas and modes of teaching that you wish to propose. As described in the following chapter, you may wish to work with and through your local communications and marketing team in order to do this research, and/or to buy in additional expertise. You are likely to need a mixed team of expertise in order to carry out this exercise thoroughly, including educational and academic experts with the market research professionals.
- Partnerships and competitors
  This activity relates to the market research activity, and will probably follow on from it, although you may be able to start some initial analysis that runs in parallel to the market research. The aim of this activity is to get a clear picture of the most relevant possible partners with whom you may wish to work in order to successfully deliver your MOOC. This may include a wide range of types of partners: the large MOOC providers; other smaller possibly local platforms; software companies; publishers; other "third-leg" industries such as charities, local public organizations, and cultural institutions; as well as other

universities and private educational providers. It is worthwhile to explore the existing university partners in the first instance, as many institutions work with a wide range of different organizations who may be interested in developing a new dimension to the partnership such as co-development of a MOOC.

During this process, you will also be able to analyze your current and potential future competitors. This will be important for the future planning process, as it may provide useful material that you can use not only to benchmark against (e.g., to identify whether you are making better progress than your main competitor) but also to understand new competitors who you may not have really considered before, such as other universities which are geographically remote from you but developing MOOCs in similar subject areas. You will want to draw up a mapping of your competitors and revise it over time, as your MOOC strategy and implementation develops, particularly as a current competitor may be a potential partner in the future.

Stage 2: planning

- **Developing your MOOC plan**
  Once you have completed Stage 1, you will have gathered a sense of the landscape in which you are operating, and be ready to begin planning in earnest. The four activities outlined below need to be carried out in parallel rather than sequentially, as far as possible.
  - Stakeholder engagement
    There is a potentially long list of stakeholders whom you may wish to engage in the development of your MOOC plan. You will want to be realistic about this process, particularly if you are planning a small-scale experiment in the first instance. It may be useful to split your list of stakeholders into two groups: key stakeholders (those who are essential to the successful delivery of the project) and other stakeholders (those whom you wish to engage but who are not essential to the process).

    As a minimum, the key stakeholders are those whose input you will need in order to develop a suitable MOOC strategy, including those who direct essential resources, and those who own and champion key, related plans and strategies. You will also want to engage with any owners of resources that will be essential to the development and delivery of the MOOC; however, it may not be clear exactly whom this will involve until you have made some progress on strategy development. This may include heads of particular academic departments.

    The initial stakeholder engagement will focus upon those stakeholders who are needed to develop the MOOC strategy. You will also need to consider how you will engage with your stakeholders during the development and delivery of the MOOC, and be aware that the key participants are likely to change over time. For example, you may want to engage local students in helping to test MOOCs once you have an initial prototype of the course in place, rather than discuss the concept of MOOCs with them, as the target audience is not likely to be local students in the first place (although it may be, depending upon your MOOC design).
- **Development of strategy and business case (costings and business models)**
  Your institutional decision-making processes are likely to guide the documentation that you need to produce in order to achieve approval for your MOOC project. Regardless of your institutional processes, experience with MOOC development indicates that it is essential to create as a minimum a strategic document to describe what you hope to achieve from your MOOC project, in terms of vision and objectives. This is important in order to achieve

a shared sense of understanding about what the MOOC project will involve and why it is important, and also to provide objectives against which you can measure the success or otherwise of the project.

It is likely that a business case of some kind will be needed before the project is approved for funding by institutional decision makers. Chapters 12 and 13 provide detailed guidance on the main resources that are needed for MOOC development and delivery, and possible business models to sustain the MOOC, that you may either wish to put in place immediately or, perhaps more likely at this early stage in MOOC maturity, to test out during the MOOC project.

You may have in place local processes for business case development that you will need to follow. If not, we refer you to PRINCE(2) and MSP that include templates and other guidance on the development of a business case (MSP, 2014).

- **Governance and management**
  Your stakeholder engagement will involve working out the key influencers and other actors who need to be involved in order to run a successful project. You need to formally determine the governance arrangements for your project, and think carefully about who will be involved in decision making (where you are at liberty to make these decisions). It is sensible to develop a draft plan for governance at this stage in the project, so that you can begin to plan key events, such as steering group meetings, well in advance of the project start date. Experience shows that a project timetable can easily be derailed by problems with getting stakeholders together in order to make decisions.

  At this stage, the team should develop a draft plan for the management of the project. As the case studies show, there are numerous different approaches for how the MOOC will be developed, depending upon the local context and also whether you plan to engage with partners as part of the development and/or deliver (such as working through a MOOC platform). If the team does not have experience of managing complex IT projects, it is recommended that there is consultation with local experts, or specialist advice sought, to draft a plan. Bear in mind that you are likely to need to bring in expertise from the legal departments and library, as well as academic departments and IT. More guidance on planning resources is given in the next chapter.

- **Development plan**
  By the end of Stage 2, the project will have received sign-off and approval to go ahead. Assuming that it is likely to be approved, you will want to preempt the decision point by starting planning the MOOC development and creating the Development Plan. There may be guidance in place locally to recommend or mandate a specific project management methodology, perhaps through the Planning Office. If not, we recommend that you use another local planning approach that has been tried and tested, or adopt a well-respected approach that is appropriate for your situation. This may include project management approaches such as PRINCE(2). If you are putting in place a large-scale and complex MOOC project, which will involve considerable stakeholder engagement and change management, you may consider that you are running a program rather than a single project, and should consider a benefits-driven methodology such as the MSP methodology. "Programme Management may be defined as the co-ordinated organization, direction and implementation of a portfolio of projects and activities that together achieve outcomes and realise benefits that are of strategic importance" (MSP, 2014).

  Whatever approach you chose, you need to ensure that the intended benefits of the project are articulated clearly in the strategy and explored in the business case (discussed in more detail in the next section).

Stage 3: running the MOOC project

Implementation of the MOOC project will follow approval of the project definition; this is now the time to put in place the MOOC project plan. The precise contents of the MOOC project plan will depend upon which project management approach you are following. It is recommended that you include the following sections in your project plan as a minimum, bearing in mind that the level of detail and complexity of your plan should be commensurate with the scale of enterprise that you are planning, whether you are development just one or two MOOCs or a more significant enterprise.

- **MOOC project plan**
  The heart of the MOOC development plan is what might be described as the project plan: the set of activities undertaken to create the MOOC or MOOCs. This plan should follow a standard project development approach, with a set of activities or work packages that are sequenced against a timeline. Whatever tools or techniques you use, the aim is to clearly articulate the key activities to be undertaken, by whom and when, so that the project manager and management group are able to monitor the project's progress

  The plan should include details of the planned development and testing model for how the MOOC(s) will be created, tested, updated, and launched.
- **Benefits identification (benefits statement)**
  Most up-to-date project management approaches advocate a benefits-driven approach; that is, where you initially identify and record the benefits that you wish to achieve by completion of the project. In the language of the PRINCE(2) project management methodology, benefits are recorded in a benefits statement. Benefits identification is useful and important because it makes it easier to ensure that the project remains aligned to the initial strategic objectives. The plan should describe benefits as precisely as possible so that their achievement can be clearly monitored and measured. As was revealed through the case studies, universities may identify a range of different drivers for involvement with MOOCs. One example would be for the university to have an increased international profile in Asia. When described as an intended benefit, this might perhaps be worded as something like "10% increase in applications from Asian countries for postgraduate courses in business studies." On the other hand, your goal may be to achieve some more general benefits, such as "to inform the university's strategy for online learning," but even in this case, you still need to articulate the benefits clearly so that you can get formal agreement from your key sponsors that they describe the purpose of the project.

  The definition of benefits is not easy and it can be fairly challenging to try to envisage the change that may occur from a specific project, particularly in an organizational culture where projects may often be focused more upon "what" rather than "why" and driven by new products or solutions rather than a clearly articulated benefit or business case. It is however, in the interest of the lead project advocate to define benefits, as otherwise it can be difficult to prove that a project has achieved what was intended.
- **Stakeholder engagement, including engagement in partnerships**
  The stakeholder engagement plan is a key part of the project plan. As described above, it is essential to engage the right stakeholders in order to deliver the MOOC project to time and to date. Identification of the most important stakeholders will depend upon the local context but is likely to include those who will be involved in sponsorship of the project, in the development of content, in management of the project, and in marketing and promotion. It should include management of partnerships, as an essential part of many MOOC projects, where partners may include a wide range of stakeholders such as the MOOC platform, providers of a technical solution, commercial partners, or other institutions.

- **Human resources**
  The development plan or project should include details of who is responsible for which activity within the project plan. It is recommended that you also formally define the roles in the project, in order to achieve complete clarity about who has responsibility for which activity. This should include reporting activities such as writing project reports as well as the delivery of each work package. It is recommended that you take a team-based approach to the development of MOOCs as bringing in the expertise of a group of people with different strengths is likely to lead to a better quality output and, when managed well, will be more efficient. "A great deal of coordination and collaboration among researchers, instructional designers, and programmers will be necessary to result in meaningful improvements to teaching and learning" (Hollands & Terthali, 2014).
- **Budget**
  Budget is one of the most important aspects of your project plan. We have included a template to help you to estimate costings in the following chapter; this can be used for an initial analysis of costs, but you will want to prepare a more detailed and refined version for approval by the appropriate part of the governance process, the steering group, or equivalent.
- **Evaluation and quality assurance**
  Evaluation and quality assurance are essential for even a small project, although they should, of course, be proportionate with the level of resource and the size of project. As a minimum, evaluation and quality assurance should be articulated in the project definition.
- **Technology options**
  This is an optional section; for some projects, where the intention is to work with an established MOOC platform, there may not be any choices to make about technology options. For others, there may need to be a detailed and costed analysis of technical solutions which follows good practice.

References

Hollands, F. M., & Terthali, D. (2014). *MOOCs: Expectations and reality. Educause*. Online at http://www.educause.edu/library/resources/moocs-expectations-and-reality.

MSP. (2014). *Welcome to the official MSP website. MSP*. Online at http://www.msp-officialsite.com.

Planning your MOOC—costings 13

This chapter sets out guidance about the costs of developing and running Massive Open Online Courses (MOOCs). Some of the early MOOC developers, such as the University of Edinburgh and FutureLearn, have shared their estimates for the costs of creating MOOCs. These are between £30,000 and £50,000 per MOOC.

These estimates are helpful but are ballpark figures that may vary widely depending upon a whole range of factors, including the subject area, the pedagogic model for the course upon which the MOOC is based, the starting state of the materials that are being used and the level of experience of the development team. Each MOOC will have a different context and will therefore require its own planning and costings.

The analysis uses the MOOC model that was examined earlier as a way to break down and analyze the cost lines for MOOC development. It analyses costs for each of the four categories in turn: interactive learning environment; learner background and intentions; technology infrastructure; evidence-based improvement. It also looks as the costs that will be incurred when creating more than one MOOC.

1. Interactive learning environment (content, instruction (or pedagogy) assessment and community)

   The main costs incurred in the interactive learning environment are for:

- creation of content, or adaptation of existing resources so that they are suitable for a MOOC environment—which may be distinctly different from the use to which the content has been put previously. The costs of creating video can be particularly high. Content creation costs need to include the salary costs for the MOOC creation team;
- instruction costs—this may include the costs of academic experts plus other support staff, such as teaching assistants. You may also need to include specialist support, such as learning technologists, and administrative support, for organizing assignments etc.
- quality assurance—this may include the cost of testing.

Content creation

It is difficult to accurately estimate the costs of creating MOOC content, without doing some analysis of the local situation and the starting point for the MOOC development. This is also the case generally when creating multimedia material and Web sites, because in both cases there are factors involved which make the costs difficult to predict accurately.

In the case studies, it was clear that cost for the creation of MOOC content was frequently difficult to predict accurately. At this early stage of MOOC development, universities tend to set aside a budget for MOOCs, and work within that budget, rather than trying to estimate costs precisely. A particular stumbling block is that it can be slow and complex to redesign or adapt materials, even where some or all of the materials are in a digital format. Quality is clearly an important issue when designing learning and teaching materials; for example, recent research shows that it is more effective for learners where you create digital video from scratch than if you reuse digital videos that were created for another purpose (Guo et al., 2014).

The university may already have costing models for developing multimedia materials, and for the creation and editing of digital video, in particular. This provides a useful starting point as it is likely to be one of the major content creation costs, if you are adopting a standard MOOC model.

Added to this, the highest costs here are likely to be the costs of staff time to create, test, and quality assure the other learning content, such as learning assessments, and to construct discussion areas and provide the overview materials for the course. This will require input from different role-holders. In the case studies, there were various approaches taken as to how the MOOC content was developed, sometimes taking a team-based approach, or having an academic lead who designed the course and other specialists also contributing to the course. The approach that you take will probably be guided by your local learning technology experts and may work with their usual resource models, or you may set up a dedicated team.

Copyright clearance and legal advice

Copyright is a particular issue in the creation and adaptation of new MOOCs—and a cost centre that is often overlooked or underestimated when predicting costs. In several of the interviews that were carried out, copyright emerged as a barrier to progress and in some cases, it delayed the planned launch date for the MOOC.

Before a MOOC is approved for development, it is recommended that an analysis of the copyright status of the materials is carried out, in order to get a clear picture of the likely status of key materials. Given the public and open nature of MOOCs, it is likely that the university legal team will not sign off a MOOC for launch unless all copyright arrangements are resolved. So a picture of possible copyright issues should be developed as early as possible in order to build in sufficient time to sort out any issues. Copyright clearance can be a very slow process and may affect overall timescales, or even prevent the launch of the MOOC if it has not been satisfactorily resolved.

Provision for expert advice on copyright needs to be included in the MOOC plan and costed properly, as it can be expensive to source, and it is easy to underestimate how much time will be needed, particularly to clear copyright for multimedia materials.

Some particularly unexpected issues with copyright that emerged in the institutions that were interviewed for this book were:

- the complexity of trying to use licensed materials: where licensing arrangements were in place for the same materials to be made available to registered students at the university, it proved difficult or impossible within the timescales to extend the licenses to MOOC students;

- it was assumed that for video materials that had been created by the institutions themselves, copyright issues would be straightforward. However, advice from the local legal team in one case was that the university could not include any branded items (such as products bearing logos) in the film clip. This meant that some videos had to be refilmed, adding weeks to the development time as well as additional, and unplanned, costs;
- teachers had developed their online learning materials with the assumption that all students would have access to a particular text book. The pedagogic model for the MOOC was that this assumption was not reasonable. The whole course had to be redesigned to draw upon different, openly available resources rather than relying on published textbooks. This added several months of delay and the MOOC had to be launched at a later date than planned.

Costs for legal advice and copyright clearance

In terms of the costs of copyright clearance and the associated costs of legal advice, not all universities have at this stage identified these costs separately, usually because they are carried out by university personnel who are already in place. Key staff are legal experts and library staff, the latter often having specialist expertise in understanding copyright and copyright clearance. For one institution, where copyright was particularly complex, the estimated costs of assuring copyright for three MOOCs, which included a lot of specialist legal advice, were about £40,000 (US$67,000); this is an extreme case, but it gives some indication of possible costs.

Another important copyright issue that does not relate directly to cost but is worthy of highlighting here is that of ownership or intellectual property rights. It is crucial that the institution agrees a formal policy for ownership of the MOOC content. This is discussed in detail in the Educause publication, *Copyright Challenges in a MOOC environment* (Cheverie, 2013).

Learner background and intentions—understanding the market

The main costs here are:

- those that relate to understanding the target audience for the MOOCs;
- the costs of designing the MOOC in order to best meet student needs.

Understanding your target audience

The institutions that were interviewed for the case studies had not invested significantly in market research specifically for the MOOC development. In many cases, they drew upon existing knowledge within the institution about the likely profile of the target student population. In other cases, no market research was done for their first MOOC experiments; their approach being to "get some MOOCs out there" and to discover from practical experience what kind of student population was attracted to the MOOC. In other cases, they left it to the MOOC platform to carry out market research and attempt to target particular populations. This seems to be more or less effective, but generally not very satisfactory.

We suggest that institutions should seriously consider investing in activities that help them to understand the target audience for the MOOCs. Costs do not need to be substantial: they may be able to tie this into other market research activities that are underway in the institution, and they will certainly be able to draw upon the data that they are collecting about their current student populations to inform their thinking. It is more a case of ensuring that resources are available and that someone is responsible for progressing this issue, than committing cash flow. However, if the institution wishes to invest highly strategically in MOOCs, for example, by picking one or two areas for MOOCs where they are likely to attract fee-paying students to related courses, then we suggest that it is worth considering making an investment of at least £10,000 (US$17,000) in this area and buying in specialist expertise if it is needed.

Designing the MOOC to meet student needs

As referred to earlier, thought needs to be given to the learning design that is appropriate for the target audience for the MOOC, depending upon their aptitudes, attitudes, and preferences. The detail of this is discussed elsewhere; but it is worth mentioning here that in terms of cost, there may be additional requirements for expenditure, depending upon the specific learning design for the MOOC. For example, you may decide that the target audience for a scientific MOOC will find it easier to understand some key concepts if they are provided with multimedia animations of sequencing DNA. If there is no appropriate open educational resource (OER) available that meets your needs, you may be required to commission or purchase a specific multimedia resource which will place an additional call on your budget, beyond that which is allocated to the "average" MOOC. So the specifics of the learning design will affect the cost of each individual MOOC, and you may wish to provide guidance to the MOOC team about what you consider to be reasonable costs, and also build some consideration of whether the MOOC will require extra resources for its development when you are selecting the MOOCs for creation.

2. Technology infrastructure

Costs for technology infrastructure will vary widely, depending upon whether the MOOC is to be hosted by a MOOC platform, another third-party or managed locally. If planning to host locally, it is helpful to consider these costs for the whole MOOC project, rather than for each individual MOOC. So please refer to the following section where we look at additional costs.

3. Evidence-based improvement

These costs will appear both for individual MOOCs and at a meta level, for the MOOC program as a whole. The costs are discussed in detail below.

4. Project or program level costs

Management, governance, publicity, costs of participation in partnerships

5. Additional costs for the MOOC project

There is a range of other activities that need to be undertaken in order to support the MOOC project at a meta level, i.e. for all the MOOCs together, rather than for each individual MOOC, including management, governance, publicity, quality assurance processes, and partnership costs.

The costs will of course vary depending upon whether the MOOC is being wholly hosted, marketed, and managed locally, or whether some or all of the processes are being carried out by a partner or third party. We have provided an analysis of all the potential costs that would apply in most cases, and then separately indicated possible cost lines, depending upon whether the MOOC is being run in-house or not.

The three main areas of resource that are required for the higher level MOOC project or program are project management, quality assurance, and evidence-based improvement (which includes evaluation, review, and reporting).

Project management

Costs here will depend upon a number of factors. Firstly and obviously, the scale of the operation that is being set up and the target number of MOOCs to be developed. Secondly, whether there is an existing team in place that already has experience of a similar project or program. If the team is able to either be diverted to work on the MOOC project or can be scaled up, perhaps through backfilling posts as well as some recruitment, this may add value in terms of speed of start-up and existing institutional knowledge. If there is no possibility of doing this, you will need to build in recruitment costs and related time delays. It may also be possible to outsource some of the MOOC activity, such as video production, but it is unlikely that you would find it easy to outsource many activities as they relate so closely to key institutional functions like course development.

The exact makeup of the MOOC production team will vary but from the experience of those institutions that we interviewed, the most common roles required are

- project manager
- academic lead(s) for content production (these may or may not be the same individuals who teach on the MOOC)
- learning technologist
- educational developer (where this role is not covered by the learning technologists)
- multimedia expert including video production
- copyright clearance expert (may possibly be located in the library)
- legal advice.

It should be noted also that the project management will be more complex and potentially more costly as the MOOC project matures, as more MOOCs are developed, and also if MOOCs are run jointly with partners.

Quality assurance

Quality assurance costs will vary widely, depending upon the QA model that is put in place. In the institutions that we interviewed, QA processes varied in complexity, depth, and completeness. The level of resource that you invest in QA will of course depend upon the strategic importance of the MOOC to your institution. If you consider the MOOC to be an experiment, with perhaps one or two MOOCs created, and no plan to scale up within 2 years' time, you may be able to manage QA for the MOOC within the existing institutional QA frameworks.

However, if you are already committed to a long-term MOOC project, or are perhaps seeing MOOCs as one part of an overall strategic approach to online learning, then you may wish to consider a more robust and comprehensive QA model.

As outlined in one of the case studies above, one possible model for QA might include four steps:

the proposal of new MOOCs;
QA monitoring as the MOOC is developed;
testing and sign off;
evaluation and reporting.

In this case, QA includes evidence-based improvement (see below).

Evidence-based improvement

This includes evaluation, review, and reporting. We have included these activities at the level of evaluating each individual MOOC, but there will also be a cost borne at a project or program level, in particular if the university wishes to build up a longitudinal picture over time, and if it wishes to engage in continuous improvement of its MOOC offer.

At a minimum level, the MOOC team needs to identify the need to gather data about the MOOCs and the MOOC students; about costs incurred; and to gather feedback from the MOOC students so that it can be analyzed in a meaningful way. A report on the outcomes from each MOOC will be needed to report into the appropriate part of the governance structure. This may be prepared by part of the in-house team as part of the overall plan, or it may be passed to another part of the institution or to an external third party to do this. The MOOC platform may provide some analytic data, for example, about usage and student profile. However, this is likely to need further analysis and setting in context before it can be shared with others and it may require significant levels of work to make it useful and usable.

At a more extensive level, the MOOC team may wish to put in place various functions to support a full evidence-based improvement model. This will include ongoing research activities to monitor, review, and evaluate use of the MOOC and its impact.

Governance

It is important to consider the costs of governance for the MOOC project and ensure that these are included in planning. This needs to include the costs of approval processes and getting buy-in from key stakeholders in the governance arrangements as well as the obvious costs of setting up and servicing decision-making bodies, such as steering groups. It is easy to put in place short-term governance arrangements that may end up being unwieldy or costly in the long run, so governance should be reviewed periodically to ensure that it remains appropriate.

None of the institutions that we interviewed were able to provide specific figures for the costs of governance; however, many recognized that they needed to review their governance models and to consider costs as part of this.

As with project management, governance will also be more complex and potentially more costly as the MOOC project matures, as more MOOCs are developed, and also if MOOCs are run jointly with partners.

Additional costs that are specific to in-house MOOCs

Platform costs

The CETIS report on MOOCs (Yuan, Powell, & Olivier, 2014) helpfully outlines three possible options for technical infrastructure.

Option 1: open up existing VLE
Option 2: MOOC platforms
Option 3: use an ad hoc platform to support innovation
To this, we might add
Option 4: use an existing external platform (such as an open source product)

The four options can be reordered to represent the balance of external versus internal resource that will be required for each.

Option 1: open up existing VLE (highest level of internal resource required)
Option 2: use an existing external platform
Option 3: use an ad hoc platform to support innovation
Option 4: MOOC platforms (lowest level of internal resource required)

As discussed in the CETIS report, cost is not the only consideration when deciding which of these options to choose.

The comparison of these four options will consider similar factors to any discussion about whether to develop and host internal systems versus the costs of outsourcing. Some of the specific issues that may arise are described below. These relate to the implications of the platform choice more generally and not only to cost, as cost has to be considered within a broader context.

For option 1, there are risks associated with opening up an existing internal platform to an external audience and also questions to ask about how much investment it is sensible to make in a single implementation of a platform, compared with being able to reap the benefits of investment in development by others. However, against this is the added value of being able to retain more control of the platform and to make decisions about its development path.

Option 2 is a good choice for experimentation, when you are not yet sure of your future MOOC strategy and do not yet wish to commit to a particular choice of technologies, nor to invest a lot of resource in choosing and perhaps customizing a set of ad hoc tools. You need to ensure that it will be possible to move the MOOC to another platform in the future, if this is possible.

Option 3 is a great choice if you are committed to an innovative approach to MOOCs and wish to invest time and effort in choosing a tool or tools and ensuring that they can be used together as part of the course. There are risks associated with using this kind of approach, as their availability and robustness may not be guaranteed, and this could potentially jeopardize the MOOC, particularly if you recruit a lot of students. This option may work best if you are openly and explicitly engaging your student body in a more experimental experience, than for a standard MOOC.

Option 4 may, of course, only be available to some institutions, as membership of platforms is not necessarily open to all. There are many advantages to this option, again not all associated with cost. In particular the associated reach and scale of the marketing activity that goes with membership of one of the large platforms can bring significant advantages to those who join. Also, there are advantages associated with the level of investment that the platform owners are making in developing the MOOC technology. However, balanced against this may be issues related to lack of autonomy and copyright ownership. Also, membership of a platform brings its own costs; these are discussed below.

Publicity and marketing

There are likely to be additional costs incurred from the promotion and marketing of the MOOC or MOOCs. As with many of these cost items, there will be a cost for each MOOC that is produced and an additional cost for promoting the University's provision of MOOCs as a new or ongoing activity.

It may be possible to meet the costs for publicity and marketing from within existing institutional budgets, but it is important to work with the communications and marketing team to ascertain whether this is the case, and if not, to be able to estimate the appropriate level of activity that may be needed and what level of cost would be associated with it. Depending upon the scale of operation, you may need to consider recruiting new staff, or outsourcing the work, or negotiating with local experts to provide the support that is needed.

The costs will vary depending on whether you are hosting your MOOC(s) yourself or are working through an existing MOOC platform or provider—or whether you are using both approaches. If you are working with a MOOC platform which will market your MOOCs through their promotional channels, you should also consider developing your own communications and marketing strategy for the MOOC(s), as you may want to target audiences who will not receive publicity through the platform's promotional channels, such as specific groups of postgraduate students or your alumni.

The strategy may draw heavily upon your usual strategies for promoting new courses to potential students and their families, but you should consider that your audience is potentially much larger and diverse. It is very early days to really understand the potential audience for MOOCs but it is clear that we should not make any assumptions about who may be interested in a particular MOOC. Potential students may not be interested in formal qualifications nor fit a particular age, gender, or educational profile. As noted above, it is worthwhile to use some resource to carry out a thorough audience analysis as part of the market research, and you should still be prepared to be surprised by who may sign up for which MOOC.

Additional costs from working with an external MOOC platform

Although working with an external MOOC platform can bring real benefits in terms of limiting costs, there will be some specific, additional costs incurred by working through one of the established MOOC platforms such as Coursera or edX, as the platforms usually charge a fee to host the MOOC on their platform. They may also charge for additional services such as quality assurance. Information about the costs associated with particular platforms varies and is always subject to discussion and individual negotiation with the platform provider. Information about the financial models for the main platforms is given in the next chapter (Table 13.1).

Table 13.1 Checklist: budget items to include when estimating costs

Budget item	Estimated cost per MOOC ($, euro, or £)
1. Market research—understanding your target audience	
2. MOOC design	
3. Content creation	
4. Copyright assurance and clearance	
5. Legal advice	
6. Technical infrastructure	
7. Management costs—project management	
8. Quality assurance	
9. Evidence-based improvement (evaluation etc.)	
10. Governance	
11. (a) Additional costs that are specific to in-house MOOCs (platform costs etc.)	
Or	
11. (b) Additional costs that are incurred by working with partner platforms	
12. Publicity and marketing	
13. Other costs incurred	
Total:	

References

Cheverie, J. (2013). *Copyright challenges in a MOOC environment*. Educause, Online at http://www.educause.edu/library/resources/copyright-challenges-mooc-environment.

Guo, P.J., Kim, J. & Rubin, R. (2014). *How video production affects student engagement: An empirical study of MOOC videos*. Online at http://pgbovine.net/publications/edX-MOOC-video-production-and-engagement_LAS-2014.pdf.

Yuan, L., Powell, S., & Olivier, W. (2014). *Beyond MOOCs: Sustainable online learning in institutions*. Centre for Educational Technology, Interoperability and Standards, Online at http://publications.cetis.ac.uk/2014/898.

Business models for MOOCs

14

The creation of sustainable business models for massive open online courses (MOOCs) is one of the most discussed and contentious issues that have arisen so far in MOOC history. The initial MOOC developments that have taken place have in many cases been funded by either venture capital or by grants from institutions or foundations. Much of the work that has been done has been openly experimental and although the major platforms claim confidence about their ability to recoup costs through a range of different business models, evidence of this is, at present, scant.

The picture is made more complex because the motivation for providing MOOCs is varied and, as we have seen in the case studies, a single university will describe a range of different motivations for providing MOOCs, all of which are being tested out at the same time. This tends to muddy the waters and makes it difficult to identify many examples of clear cost–benefit analysis.

However, there is an emerging body of experience, not least in those institutions that were interviewed as part of the research for this publication. There is certainly a great deal more clarity about the costs of developing and providing MOOCs than was previously available, and also as more MOOCs have been planned, created, and launched, there is more detail that can be shared about the motivation for MOOCs and what has been discovered so far about the business models that may underpin them.

As we know, initial investment in the first MOOC platforms has come from two main sources: either venture capital from the commercial sector (for Coursera and Udacity) or investment from universities and foundations (for edX and FutureLearn). This investment has been made with the assumption that, at some point, it will be possible to put in place sustainable business models that will work effectively both for the MOOC platforms and for their partners.

The MOOC platforms have openly discussed the kinds of revenue streams that they expect to tap into, based upon the "freemium" model—where content is provided for free, and charges are made for optional, 'premium' services.

We summarize below the main "monetization" options that are being tested out by the main MOOC platforms. The main models that are being used currently are:

- charged-for certification—generally costing around £30 or US$50;
- secure assessments—a more stringent level of testing and certification, generally costing around £90 or US$150;
- charges for recommending third-party services, for example, directing students to Amazon books.

Other models that are also being explored but are at an earlier stage of maturity are:

- licensing of MOOC content to other educational institutions, for example, to use in delivering credit-bearing courses;
- employee recruiting—brokering links between MOOC students and potential employers;
- tutoring services to give personal support to MOOC students.

Below, we summarize the current business models that are being explored by the main MOOC platforms, and identify the financial benefits that a university partner can expect to receive from them.

Udacity business models

Udacity started out by experimenting with the same business models as the other main players, expecting to recoup investment through certification and selling "premium" services to students. However, in late 2013, Udacity decided to fundamentally refocus its activities to concentrate upon working with the corporate training market, rather than working with universities (Chafkin, 2013).

Udacity has committed to continuing to provide content to students freely, but concentrating its development upon charged-for services such as tutoring, testing and accreditation, and sponsored partnerships with training providers. As noted earlier, its most radical educational experiment to date has been to partner with Georgia Tech University and the telecoms provider, AT&T, to offer a master level degree in computer science at a greatly reduced price when compared to its equivalent traditional, on-campus experience (Onlink, 2013).

What is in it for the university partner?

The details of the financial arrangements between Udacity, its commercial and academic partners have not been made available publically. Given this change in direction, it seems unlikely that Udacity will offer many opportunities for universities and colleges in the future, other than for a select few who match the limited criteria that Udacity demands. So their business models are less directly relevant to our discussion here.

It will, however, be very interesting and informative to observe the success or failure of their new approaches, particularly as they blur the boundaries around free and open courses and test out some innovative business models working with different types of partners.

Coursera monetization options

These monetization options are those that Coursera has publically stated will be explored by them and that may form part of current and future routes to income generation. This list is taken from a sample contract that has been made available to the public through the Chronicle of Higher Education's Web site, and which was drafted for the University of Michigan.

> "Coursera Monetization Options
> Certification
> Secure assessments
> Employee recruiting
> Employee or university screening
> Human-provided tutoring or manual grading
> Corporate/university enterprise model
> Sponsorships Tuition fees" (Young, 2012)

What is in it for the university partner?

For each of these models, the platform provider will take the largest proportion of the income. Precise figures depend upon the arrangements that are put in place, as Coursera enters into specific contractual arrangements with each university partner on an individual basis. However, from analysis of the arrangements that have been put in place to date with Coursera's partners, the partner's proportion of income generated through these models described above is usually between 6% and 15% of income. More recently, Coursera has announced that it will offer an additional, charged-for service called 'Specializations', where a student can take a set of MOOCs that follow a particular subject area, and use them to get credit for a more substantial qualification (Kolowich, 2014). Coursera is looking to work with commercial organisations, such as Google, to accredit these qualifications with a capstone course (Lapowski, 2015). It is not yet clear what the implications of this will be for universities.

edX financial arrangement options

EdX is experimenting with two different financial arrangements for how it works with its partners.

> Option A: the University Self-service Model

In the self-service model, courses are created by the university partner with no course creation input from edX. Courses are not quality assured by edX either, so they are branded as "Edge" courses rather than full edX courses, until an edX quality assurance process has been carried out.

What is in it for the university partner?

Under the self-service model, there is no charge made to the institution for inclusion of their course on the edX platform until income is generated. When income is generated, edX receives the gross revenue from the course up to $US50,000 for each new course that is offered. For each time the course is repeated, edX will receive an additional $US10,000.

Beyond this income level, that is, once the first $US50,000 have been made, the university will keep 50% of any additional gross revenue.

Option B: the edX-Supported Model

In the edX-supported model, course production is supported by edX in return for a payment to edX of $US250,000 per course. There is also a charge of an additional $US50,000 for each time that the course is offered.

What is in it for the university partner?

If the university uses only this model, it will receive a minimum of 70% of any income generated.

There are other arrangements in place where the University can choose to combine the two models, or can choose to switch between them. In each case, a different model will apply for how income is calculated.

A sample edX contract is available online at http://chronicle.com/article/Document-The-Revenue-Sharing/137429/.

FutureLearn business models

FutureLearn's public statements about business models have been that it will be focusing in the first instance upon the needs of learners and partners, in order to create "an excellent product" and that they fully expect sustainable business models to arise because of the quality of their offer. "Producing an excellent product is our primary motivation. In an evolving market, the development of sustainable business models is always a challenge but I believe that if we build something great, a whole range of business opportunities could come our way" (FutureLearn, 2013).

More specifically, FutureLearn is experimenting with some of the same models that the other platforms are using. This includes charging for certification, where students who have completed at least 50% of the MOOC are able to buy a Statement of Participation which is signed by the lead academic on the course, for £24 (US$40).

FutureLearn is also experimenting with proctored examinations, where the student takes an examination based upon the content of the MOOC, set by the partner university, at an examination center that is local to them. The service is run by an experienced third-party provider, the global testing network Prometric, through its over 10,000 examination testing centers which are spread across the globe, in 160 countries. The current charge to students for this service is £119 (US$200).

What is in it for the university partner?

FutureLearn is taking a different approach from the "big three" in terms of the model that they are using to give a share of revenue to their university partners. Their current approach is to reward financially those institutions that attract students and where students complete the MOOCs. Universities that run MOOCs where high numbers of people register and complete the MOOCs will receive a higher percentage of revenue (not income) is generated through certification and other services. There is a sliding scale of revenue returned to the university partner depending upon the success of its MOOC when it is ranked with all other FutureLearn MOOCs. The scale varies from about 20% of revenue generated, for the top 10% of MOOCs, to 10% of revenue generated, for the least popular MOOCs.

This is an innovative business model and it will be very interesting to see how successful it is, both for generating reasonable income for its university partners, and also for the sustainability of FutureLearn itself.

Partners of FutureLearn comment upon the interesting challenges that lie ahead for FutureLearn in becoming sustainable. It seems unlikely that FutureLearn will ever attract the very high number of users that use Coursera, for example, as they have already got market lead, brand awareness, and high market share. So business models that depend upon selling premium services, like accreditation and examination, to small percentages of very large numbers of students, will not scale up as well for FutureLearn and other platforms, and the figures may simply not add up. It is likely to be a similar situation for some of the other, emerging MOOC platforms.

Given these conditions, and as the MOOC market continues to develop and mature, it will be interesting to observe whether the FutureLearn partners decide to "stay local" and stay with FutureLearn, if they are also offered the opportunity to join one of the other platforms, which can perhaps offer access to far greater numbers of potential students. Equally, will the restrictions placed upon the FutureLearn partners that arise naturally from being part of a large consortium, for example, having to use a particular platform with its specific models for how learning is supported and how content is hosted, be perceived by some as too restrictive, perhaps leading some of the more confident partners to either set up their own MOOCs, or to work with other partners (including a range of nonuniversity and commercial partners)?

We also should bear in mind that FutureLearn is a commercial entity and not part of the not-for-profit university sector, and as a commercial operation it will have its own motivation for making decisions about its current and future business, and which of many possible business models it chooses to pursue. It is reasonable to assume that at some point, these may not align entirely with those of some or all of its partners. So it is likely that we will see flux and change in the membership of FutureLearn—and indeed, of all the large MOOC platforms—as experience grows and business models are refined.

One thing is certain at the current time is that the FutureLearn partnership has already proven itself to be a highly successful collaboration between a diverse group of institutions that are generally more likely to be competing with each other rather than collaborating, certainly on such a public and large-scale venture. We are perhaps seeing a maturing of awareness and understanding in the leadership of some universities, which recognizes that although competition is a strong and perhaps necessary part of the current global higher education ecology, it is possible to combine collaboration with competitors, such that it brings benefits to all parties.

As discussions about cost reduction and sustainability of higher education institutions continue over the coming years, it will be fascinating to see whether this kind of mature relationship may lead to other shared ventures in the online learning sphere, and also in related areas, such as shared services, collaboration around curriculum, facilities, and so on. There is a great deal of potential here but the requirement for some new approaches to partnership and business models has to date mostly prevented a high level of collaboration. Experts such as Tony Bates are discussing the competing forces that make collaboration around online learning so challenging (e.g., see Bates, 2014).

Revenue generation options for universities who provide MOOCs

Offering accreditation

Accreditation is clearly one of the key areas of interest and potential stumbling blocks for institutions, particularly when the protection of the university brand and its core offer are of such primary importance to many.

Early though we are in the genesis of MOOCs, we have already been able to observe a whole set of misconceptions about accreditation that has been rehearsed, tested, and then disproven. The original assumptions of many, including leaders of the major MOOC platforms, were that accreditation would be a major influence and differentiating factor for MOOC students, who would have a strong motivation to be accredited for their MOOC learning, and that this would naturally create a significant income stream for the platforms and their partners.

Through 2012 and into 2013, as evaluation data from MOOC students and take up rates for the new certification and accreditation offers became known, it became clear that these were not proving to be the main motivation for most MOOC learners, and indeed were seen as more or less irrelevant by many.

As we saw in the case studies, accreditation is an issue that all MOOC providers are considering, but that most are treating carefully as the likely level of take up in the future is so unclear.

Charges for certification

Many universities are comfortable with providing charged-for certification, through a "statement of achievement," "statement of accomplishment," "certification of completion," or similar. This will generally be made available to the students if they have completed more than a specific proportion of the MOOC course and attempted at least some of the assessments. The certificate will probably include details of the course taken and the name of the university, and may be signed by the lead educator. In general, universities are comfortable with this arrangement and, as described above, they receive some financial benefits from it.

Accreditation

Accreditation is a different issue. In almost all cases, accreditation will come from the platform and not from the university. Where this is provided by the MOOC platform rather than the institution, the university will usually receive a small percentage of the income generated. Most institutions are comfortable with this model because it does not threaten to undermine the quality of their brand or compete directly with their traditional, accredited courses.

Any university that plans to accredit online learning itself needs to think carefully about the pros and cons of this, to plan carefully for appropriate quality assurance procedures, and to consider the possible impact on its existing income streams. As several universities noted during interviews, it is very important to their strategy to keep a clear divide between their traditional, accredited courses and MOOCs, at least at this stage of development.

Proctored examinations and other forms of summative assessment

A further option that can be made available is to offer formally proctored examinations. In most cases, these will be offered through a third-party service provider rather than by the university or MOOC platform itself. There is a range of service providers that are able to provide this option to universities. Universities will need to include planning for the setting and marking of the examinations in their planning processes. Income generation from formal examinations needs to cover the costs of using third-party services for proctoring.

So we can see from this analysis that there are various approaches to certification and accreditation that can be put in place that will lead to income generation for the institution. Income levels will clearly depend upon the level of take-up by MOOC students, and data about take-up is still inconclusive.

Beyond these obvious business models, there are other income generation models that may apply, where the institution may access the benefit of creating and providing a MOOC. We have provided a summary of some of the main models that are being explored currently in the next chapter.

Converting MOOC students to fee-paying courses

This model is one that is being tested and explored by many of the institutions that are currently engaged with MOOCs and is a model that is often cited as one of the potential (though, as yet, largely unproven) possible benefits that MOOCs may bring. It features in the case studies that we have included in this book as a model that is being explored by many different types of institutions, and one which seems to be proving itself as successful. There is limited evidence to date about the level at which the level of conversion from a MOOC student to a fee-paying student is occurring at a level which would justify the investment in the MOOC, but there are some examples that are worth referring to and examining.

The **University of London** (UoL) began to offer MOOCs through the Coursera platform in 2013. It is one of the few MOOC providers that has written up its first MOOC experiences into a published report, and as such is a valuable source of intelligence.

UoL states that one of its explicit aims in terms of business models was to explore the conversion of students from its MOOCs to undergraduate courses. In its September

2013 report, it states that "just under 35 students have indicated on their University of London International Programmes application form that they took one of our four MOOCs before applying for a full degree programme" (Grainger, 2013). These students were attracted from over 210,000 initial registrations, which translated into 90,000 students who were active in their first week.

These statistics need, of course, to be looked at in the context that the students are self-reporting and may not represent all of those who applied for the University of London International Programmes; nor can they include students who may subsequently apply for UoL programmes. They also need to be looked at in the context of what level of conversion the UoL would consider to be sufficient to meet their sustainability needs, for example, whether they would seek to completely cover all MOOC production costs through increased enrollment and whether they would seek to cover costs in one instantiation of the MOOC or spread the costs over a number of reruns of the MOOC. However, looked at starkly, the conversion rates represent a very small percentage of successful conversion and the income generated seems unlikely to cover anything but a small proportion of the costs incurred in MOOC production. We should bear in mind also that the University of London International programme is an experienced provider of online and distance learning, having run distance-learning courses since the nineteenth century, and as such is in a stronger position to market its undergraduate programmes to a MOOC audience than many other institutions.

The **University of Tasmania**, has been successful in recruiting students to its "Understanding Dementia" MOOC, (http://www.utas.edu.au/wicking/wca/mooc), which has run several times and recruited over 10,000 students. What has been particularly interesting about this MOOC is that it has seen very high levels of student retention, with nearly 40% of registrants completing the MOOC—substantially higher than on most MOOCs, which typically see completion rates of up to 10%, and often only around 5–7%. Following the first completed MOOC a significant percentage then transferred to the fully online Bachelor in Dementia Care which is a fee-charged, fully online course.

This example is particularly useful because the "Understanding Dementia MOOC" is offered directly by the University of Tasmania, rather than through a MOOC platform. So one conclusion that we can draw from this example is that if a university offers specialist MOOCs in an area of strength, and particularly where they have a strong online offer, then the conversion rate may be high.

These are just two examples of business models that are at least partly based upon the conversion of students. As we have noted, MOOCs are at an immature stage of development and it is premature to draw too many conclusions from the experience to date. However, we can see that already there is some potential to encourage student applications for fee-paying courses by offering them the opportunity to participate in related, free, and open courses in a MOOC format.

Benefits of engaging with students through MOOCs

Perhaps more compellingly, if we think about the longer term, there are potentially more sophisticated approaches to engaging with students through the MOOC that may hold real benefits to both student and university. These benefits might include helping students to understand more about the subject that they are interested in studying and how it is taught at this particular institution, which might lead to better match between student and course and hence lower dropout rates. There is also the possibility of some level of "prescreening," where participation in the MOOC is used to support the student's eventual application to a formal course, and may even form part of the evidence for their application. Clearly, there are many issues to think through around the second model in particular, but there are possibilities here that it will be useful to consider as MOOCs mature, and in particular as we are able to use data collection and analytics to understand more about the choices that students are making about university applications.

Some of these models are beginning to be explored by universities in practice.

The **University of Sheffield**, for example, is running a MOOC called "Discover Dentistry" which is aimed specifically at people who are considering applying to study dentistry at university, and explicitly wants to help potential students to apply for dentistry courses, with the aim to "reach even more students, potentially equipping thousands of aspiring dentists from around the world for their dental school application" (Belfast Telegraph, 2014).

References

Bates, T. (2014). *Why successful consortia for online learning are so difficult.* Online Learning and Distance Education Resources moderated by Tony Bates. Online at http://www.tonybates.ca/2014/04/12/why-consortia-for-online-learning-are-so-difficult-to-form/#sthash.NyKQ9bUH.dpuf.

Belfast Telegraph. (2014). *Online dentistry course launched.* Belfast Telegraph Online, Online at http://www.belfasttelegraph.co.uk/breakingnews/offbeat/online-dentistry-course-launched-30076041.html.

Chafkin, M. (2013). *Udacity's Sebastian Thrun, godfather of free online education, changes course.* Fast Company, Online at http://www.fastcompany.com/3021473/udacity-sebastian-thrun-uphill-climb.

FutureLearn. (2013). *Introduction from Simon Nelson, CEO at FutureLearn.* FutureLearn, Online at https://about.futurelearn.com/feature/introduction-from-simon-nelson-launch-ceo-futurelearn/.

Grainger, B. (2013). *Massive open online course (MOOC) report.* University of London. Online at http://www.londoninternational.ac.uk/sites/default/files/documents/mooc_report-2013.pdf.

Kolowich, S. (2014). *Coursera Will Offer Certificates for Sequences of MOOCs.* The Chronicle of Higher Education. Online at http://chronicle.com/blogs/wiredcampus/coursera-will-offer-certificates-for-sequences-of-moocs/49581.

Lapowski, I. (2015). *How Coursera Is Connecting Its Students to Tech Employers Like Google.* Wired 02.11.15. Online at http://www.wired.com/2015/02/instagram-google-coursera/.

Onlink, T. (2013). *Georgia tech, Udacity shock higher ed with $7,000 degree.* Forbes.com, Online at http://www.forbes.com/sites/troyonink/2013/05/15/georgia-tech-udacity-shock-higher-ed-with-7000-degree/.

Young, J. (2012). *Inside the coursera contract: How an upstart company might profit from free courses.* Chronicle of Higher Education, Online at https://chronicle.com/article/How-an-Upstart-Company-Might/133065/.

Additional benefits of MOOCs

15

The benefits of providing Massive Open Online Courses (MOOCs) are not just about income generation; many of the benefits identified in our case studies are "softer" in nature, that is, they are predicated upon longer-term investments that may have a less certain financial outcome such building, profile raising or fulfillment of strategies for public engagement, public good, and similar objectives. These softer benefits may in time lead to substantial income generation, but this is generally less certain than for some of the approaches discussed in the last chapter.

In this chapter, we look at some of the other benefits of providing MOOCs that are commonly cited by providers and analyze some of the pros and cons of including these benefits in your MOOC planning.

Developing markets and building relationships with new customers

From the interviews that we carried out with a number of different universities, there is a strong belief that MOOCs have the potential to help market the institution better to more people, to develop a deeper and more nuanced sense of the institution's brand and identity, and also to build up more sophisticated relationships with not only actual and potential students, but also with third parties, such as parents, grandparents, cousins, friends, all of whom may play a powerful role in referring students to a particular institution.

MOOCs offer a way of lower risk and lower cost to promote the institution to a wide audience. Not only do they offer a route to promoting their name to potential students, but also enable the institution to give the MOOC student a sense of some of the areas of strength of the institution, and even perhaps a sense of their identity as an organization.

The *University of Bristol*, for example, plans to give at least one of its MOOCs a sense of Bristol as a city and the values of the University, so that through the MOOC, the student also gets a sense of some of the characteristics of living and studying in Bristol, and may be encouraged to apply to the University.

Understanding the market

As with its other marketing strategies, a university will need to understand its target markets and, where possible, try to match these with MOOCs in the most relevant subject areas. It is too early to tell whether this strategy will be successful, but indicators so far are that this approach is definitely worth investigation and trialing.

So, for example, a grandparent may take part a MOOC focused on European history because of a long-standing interest in the subject, may enjoy the course, and be highly impressed by the quality of teaching and thus feel that this has given them a personal "link" with the university that provides the MOOC, and so encourage their grandchild to consider applying to that university to study either archaeology or a completely different subject area. The investment in the MOOC will, through an indirect route and over a period of time, translate into an undergraduate application that the university would not otherwise have had.

Attracting global audiences

The potential to market to a global audience is also one of the most cited benefits to universities that offer MOOCs, and in particular to reach individuals or communities where they do not traditionally have a strong presence. As we have seen in recent years, many universities are increasingly interested in attracting overseas students, both for undergraduate and postgraduate study. Some are pursuing expensive strategies to engage with potential students, through the use of third-party agencies that engage with students, for example, or going further, by setting up overseas offices on the other side of the world. Or the university may set up a campus either in partnership with a local institution or alone.

MOOCs offer a lower cost approach to marketing abroad, and hold potential to get directly to a specific target group of potential students who may have an interest in a very specific subject area. This is particularly relevant to postgraduate courses where numbers may be small but the benefits of matching the right student to the right course may be large leading to more applications and income.

Developing new markets through more flexible courses

As discussed in the case studies, universities are not only thinking about promoting their traditional course offers, but some institutions are offering a range of more flexible models. This may include offering access to individual modules rather than an entire program, and also offering a broader range of courses that are aimed more at lifelong learners than undergraduates or postgraduates; for example, short summer school courses.

Given what we know so far about the demographics of MOOCs, one of the most strongly represented cohorts is that of lifelong learners who are interested in a subject as an enthusiast, rather than as part of their career path (one university light-heartedly described the intake for their MOOCs as being "the University of the Third Age" (U3A, 2014)). There is the possibility to blur the boundary between formal and informal learning further, and to use MOOCs to promote existing or new short courses that are specifically aimed at lifelong learners.

The *University of Southampton* is experimenting with this approach by running a MOOC that takes as its focus the Portus project, an archaeology module that is open to the public and for which there is a field study trip each summer near to Rome in Italy. By running a MOOC that also focuses upon the Portus project, greater numbers may be encouraged to engage with it and perhaps to attend the summer school (Portus Project, 2014).

Some of these courses may be credit-bearing but many will not be. The key point in planning a MOOC strategy that aims, at least in part, to engage this potential market is to understand the profile of current and future lifelong learning students, and to provide a MOOC offer that is likely to attract their attention and then to meet their needs as enthusiasts as well as learners. Their motivation for engagement in a MOOC is likely to be subtly different to that of a potential undergraduate or an employee who wishes to acquire new, job-related knowledge, and the MOOC may need to be marketed and designed accordingly.

Bespoke course development with partners

A less common MOOC model that holds possibilities for new incomes streams is that of working in partnership with other organizations to develop, run, and/or to accredit the MOOC.

An interesting example in the UK is the partnership between the *University of Exeter*, running a MOOC through the FutureLearn platform, and the Association of Chartered Certified Accountants (ACCA), a professional body that offers professional accreditation to accountants and other financial professionals. The two partners are working together to create a MOOC that will then be accredited by ACCA (Boyde, 2014).

This model is innovative because it holds the potential to attract new students and to open up new income streams for the University, but without compromising their core offer of high-quality undergraduate courses, as accreditation is offered by the partner rather than the University. It is an example of a mutually beneficial partnership, where the University brings its knowledge assets and experience of good course design and delivery, and the professional association brings specialist subject knowledge and branding. Other universities are working in partnership with commercial companies and not-for-profits, often where they have an established arrangement in place.

Conclusion

Bringing together the key points from this and the previous chapter, we can see that there are numerous ways that MOOCs may bring direct or indirect financial benefits to both MOOC platforms and to MOOC providers. However, given the early stage of maturity of MOOCs within the complex market of global higher education, these models are still largely unproven and there is, as yet, no clear model for funding MOOCs in a financially sustainable way.

Most obvious business models are linked to certification and accreditation, but take-up levels of these services so far are not particularly promising—though we have to bear in mind that the students who have so far taken MOOCs may not be representative of the population that will be seen in 5 or 10 years' time, as MOOCs move beyond the "early-adopter" phase in the innovation curve.

It can be difficult to measure the benefit of MOOCs, as there may be indirect benefits with no direct financial outcomes—or financial outcomes that take some time to reach fruition. Some of the benefits are definitely not financial but nevertheless may contribute directly to the strategy of the university, for example by attracting better quality students to postgraduate courses. Some universities hope to convert MOOC students to fee-paying students.

However, many of the reasons for providing MOOCs are not directly linked to recruitment. One of the much cited motivations for offering free online courses is a complex and sometimes rather muddled bundle of rationales that, in marketing terms, include aspects of developing brand awareness, building new or improving relationships with current and potential "customers," and marketing to new audiences. In general, these aspirations seem to reflect the marketing strategy of the university, with the MOOC providing an additional possible "route to market," and one that has particular advantages in its global reach.

There is a lot bound up in this discussion and one of the complexities is that, as with traditional marketing practices, it is difficult or sometimes impossible to trace a clear path of causality from the investment in marketing and the final "sale" to the "customer." It is for the institution to decide which of its strategic objectives it is trying to address through the provision of a MOOC, and to put in place evaluation strategies that can determine whether the MOOC has helped to achieve the objectives or not. Experience from the institutions that we interviewed indicates that the best way to find out about this is through practical experimentation, and given the fast-growing level of interest in online learning by potential students, we would strongly advise that each university develops a clear strategy that will enable it to invest in practical developments. We would also counsel engagement with other institutions in order to share practice and learn from others. Partnership in MOOC platforms is one good way to achieve this, but open and frank conversations with established partners may provide another useful route.

It should also be noted that the partnership agreements with the major MOOC platforms are nonexclusive. This means that there is no barrier to the university deciding to either run the same MOOC on another platform or to move the MOOC to another platform. At this early stage in maturity for online learning in general, and in particular for MOOCs, we advise that institutions are open minded about testing out a number of different options, if they are able to, rather than rushing to commit to one particular model, partner, or provider in the long term. The future of MOOCs is still emerging and it will be some time before the shape of the landscape becomes clear.

References

Boyde, E. (2014). *ACCA to recognise qualifying Moocs on FutureLearn*. FT.com, Online at: http://www.ft.com/cms/s/2/71ca6014-aa01-11e3-8497-00144feab7de.html#axzz2vxNkvBFY.

Portus Project. (2014). *Portus MOOC—archaeology of Portus: exploring the lost harbour of ancient Rome*. University of Southampton, Online at: http://www.portusproject.org/education/portus-mooc/.

U3A. (2014). *The University of the Third Age*. The Third Age Trust, Online at: http://www.u3a.org.uk.

Part Two

Looking to the future

Key areas for strategic investigation and decision-making

The following chapters focus upon three areas that we consider to be crucial to the successful deployment and that will lead to the best returns to the provider, including the range of potential benefits that were outlined in the previous chapter.

The three areas are:

- understanding your market: the learner as consumer;
- data and analytics;
- the developing MOOC market.

Understanding your market—the learner as consumer

16

Introduction

Much of the discussion around MOOCs has focused upon the "supplier" end of the picture: the current providers of higher education and what MOOCs may mean to them; the new organizations that have emerged to create and provide MOOC platforms; the possible new entrants into the higher education market, who may reap the benefits of the MOOC development curve in order to develop their position and market share.

While engaged in these important and interesting discussions, we should not forget that the reason that MOOCs have gained such profile and importance so quickly is because their growth has been fuelled by consumers and not by suppliers. Early MOOCs not a carefully thought-through business proposition with a clear rationale, target audience, and business model. It is the fact that consumers—or learners—have voted with their keyboards to engage with MOOCs that has led to the current multimillion pound investment in a series of unproven start-ups. Added to this is the potential brought by combining networked technologies with big data and new analytic tools. we have a unique opportunity to find out more about learners when they engage in online learning, and to adapt our educational offer to their requirements, than at any other time in the past.

It would be a mistake, though, to act as if MOOCs are being developed in a vacuum of previous broad and deep understanding of what is needed to create "good" online learning experiences. Online learning has been developing and growing over the last 20 years, with many thousands of online courses developed using a range of different technologies, tools, and pedagogic approaches. From the beginning, both teachers and those supporting online learning, specialists such as learning technologists and educational developers, have evaluated online learning and reviewed its efficacy. In the last 10 years, there has been particular emphasis on the deeper understanding of how online learning can be best constructed so as to provide the best possible learning experience. In this section, we will identify those areas of learning that are most crucial for the development of good practice in creating MOOCs that is likely to recruit and retain MOOC students, and so result in good return on investment.

Understanding learner motivation

Understanding what motivates learners to learn effectively is one of the keys to successful education, and not surprisingly, there has been detailed research into this area over many years.

More recently, research has been carried out to understand more about the motivation of learners in an online context. This research holds significant potential to help understanding of online learning, and can be particularly useful in the design of MOOCs, where motivation is such an important and unknown influence—why do some MOOCs attract hundreds of thousands of potential learners, but have very low completion rates? What attracts someone to sign up for a MOOC in the first place, and how should a provider attempt to retain their interest in the MOOC, once it has started?

This is a complex area because of the many contributing factors that are present, and there is no simple answer to the questions posed above. However, research has helpfully indicated some of the key issues that need to be addressed in considering learner motivation.

More helpfully, recent research concludes that there is a complex relationship between the learner and the learning opportunity which is influenced by a range of motivating factors—put simply, a learner may be motivated by different things and respond in different ways, depending upon what they are trying to learn, in what context, and who else they are learning with. So there are both intrinsic traits in learners and factors, in the learning environment, that will motivate the learner which can lead to either a successful or unsuccessful learning opportunity (Hartnett, St George, & Dron, 2011).

The following quote gives helpful guidance:

> *Practitioners need to be cognisant of the important role they play in influencing learner motivation when designing learning activities. Most importantly, the relevance and value of the task (e.g., online discussions) need to be clearly identified and linked to learning objectives to help learners understand how the activity can aid in the realisation of personal goals, aspirations, and interests, both in the short and longer term. By offering meaningful choices (i.e., not just option choices) to learners that allow them to pursue topics that are of interest to them, the perceived value of the activity is further enhanced. Finally, by establishing frequent, ongoing communication with learners, where they feel able to discuss issues in an open and honest manner, practitioners are in a better position to accurately monitor and respond to situational factors that could potentially undermine learner motivation.*
>
> *Hartnett et al. (2011)*

What should we take from this quote when we plan to design MOOCs? Firstly, design of the environment is very important—and here we are using a broad definition of design that encompasses the type of support and encouragement that is used, and not just the learning platform. So, for example, the use of weekly e-mails to remind the learner of their progress so far on the course and to highlight progress of their peers is one approach to increasing motivation. This relates closely to the topic of learning design, which we will discuss in more detail below.

Secondly, we need to take into account that behaviors associated with engagement with MOOCs are not simply focused upon learning attainment; the apparent lack of interest in accreditation as a major motivating factor for studying within a MOOC is evidence of this. Some of the elements that motivate learners to engage with MOOCs may be more allied to other contexts where education and entertainment come together and boundaries blur. Some of the literature that is relevant here is about consumer behaviors rather than learning behaviors—and it is perhaps no coincidence that there is a high level of engagement of marketing professionals in the teams that are choosing and creating MOOCs, who are clearly contributing their particular expertise, in understanding what attracts and engages potential consumers, into the decision-making process.

Learning design

Learning design can be described as "the description of the teaching-learning process that takes place in a unit of learning (e.g., a course, a lesson, or any other designed learning event)" (Koper, 2006). The term learning design is similar to others that are widely used in the literature of course design and pedagogy, including terms such as instructional design and curriculum design. Learning design is appropriate to our discussion because it includes the design of the whole experience—the learning objectives that will be attained, and how this will happen, including both planned instructional materials and also the associated activities that support the learning process, including learner–learner or learner–teacher interactions.

When planning online learning, it can be easy to focus upon the tools and technologies that are available and to frame the learning design around them. So, for example, the course must be planned in terms of the number of multimedia elements that will be included, and the number of topics covered, rather than starting from a point of articulating the planned learning objectives, and then analyzing the range of tools and techniques that are available that will best enable the learners to meet those objectives.

Frameworks such as the "7 Cs toolkit" have been developed in order to provide supportive structures and guidance for those who are designing learning activities (Conole, 2013a). The 7 Cs are "conceptualize, capture, create, communicate, collaborate, consider, and consolidate" and are used to underpin a set of 21 "e-tivities" which the learning designer works through in order to plan the learning experience. These have been tested out with large numbers of teachers in order to ensure that they are useful. The 7Cs toolkit is available for free use from the Beyond Distance Research Alliance (2014).

When planning MOOCs, you may be limited in choosing your learning design by the platform that you are working with, but it is still advised to support the MOOC design team—probably the academic leads, learning technologists, and perhaps educational developers, working together—to take time initially to plan out appropriate learning designs for each MOOC. It may be your wish whether to specify a particular learning design approach that will be used for all your MOOCs, or choose different learning designs for different audiences and subject areas. MOOCs are no different to other forms of online learning in that the construction of the learning sequences is just as important as the selection of content, and given how little you may know about your cohort of MOOC users, it is even more important to do all that you can to support them through the learning process.

In terms of MOOC-specific learning designs, MOOCs are sometimes characterized quite crudely as either cMOOCs or xMOOCs. As discussed earlier, cMOOCs are "Connectivist MOOCs" that use the educational theory of connectivism as their underpinning; while xMOOCs do not ascribe to an explicit pedagogic theory or model, but tend to focus on simple pedagogic models that communicate materials in an instructional way, rather than being learner focused.

xMOOCs		cMOOCs
Scalability of provision	Massive	Community and connections
Open access—restricted license	Open	Open access and license
Individual learning in single platform	Online	Networked learning across multiple platforms and services
Acquire a curriculum of knowledge and skills	Course	Develop shared practices, knowledge, and understanding

The different characteristics of xMOOCs and cMOOCs are captured clearly by Li, Powell, and Olivier (2014).

These distinctions are not very helpful, however, as the xMOOC label, in particular, is an overly simplistic way to describe a multiplicity of different practices and approaches.

Chapter 3 provides one simple way to analyze existing MOOCs in order to better understand the various aspects that need to be included in planning. A more comprehensive and pedagogically driven approach has been taken by Grainne Conole who has done valuable work to analyze MOOCs according to 10 dimensions of MOOCs (Conole, 2013). The example below shows how she has mapped five different MOOC courses against the 10 dimensions in order to analyze the approach that each MOOCs has taken. This approach can provide a useful checklist for MOOC designers against which to analyze the ambitions for a new MOOC, and to look at the design of a current MOOC. This is an evolving methodology which will be useful to monitor further as it develops (Table 16.1).

Learner support

Supporting learners online is much broader and more complex than just supporting online discussions and there is a wealth of research developed over many years in order which discusses learner support and advises upon good practice. Local learning technologists and educational specialists will be able to advise but in addition, excellent sources of guidance include work by Helen Beetham, Diana Laurillard, and Gilly Salmon.

Table 16.1 Mapping five courses to the 10 dimensions of MOOCs

Dimension	Low	Medium	High
Open		H817, OE, AI	CCK, OLDS
Massive	OLDS, H817, OE	CCK	AI
Use of multimedia		CCK, OLDS, H817, OE	AI
Degree of communication	AI	OLDS, H817, OE	CCK
Degree of collaboration	AI	CCK, OLDS, OE	H817
Learning pathway	CCK	OLDS, H817, OE	AI
Quality assurance	CCK	AI, OLDS, OE	H817
Amount of reflection	AI	OLDS, OE	CCK
Certification	CCK28	OLDS, AI	OE
Formal learning	AI, CCK	OLDS	H817, OE
Autonomy		H817, OE	CCK, OLDS, AI
Diversity		H817, AI, OLDS	

Table reproduced from Conole (2013b).

In considering what support is needed for learners in a MOOC scenario, it is important to ensure that the full breadth of support needs is considered. Online support to learners can be described in many ways; one useful suggestion is to break down online learner support into three categories: technical, academic, and study skills support (Morrison, 2014). Technical support includes helping the learner to connect to systems, to navigate the MOOC platform, and so on. The level of support that may be needed to resolve technical queries should not be overlooked, as failing to access systems is an important factor in demotivating students. A large percentage of this support is administrative support (passwords, questions about assignments) and also the broader type of interaction that goes beyond the specific activity, or assignment—where the learner feels supported as part of the learning community of the institution. Study skills support is a more general support that is available to help the student to acquire or hone their general abilities in learning online, perhaps to understand how to undertake academic work, how to plan their time and so on.

There is a lot of high quality, free guidance available to support planning online learning and the important element of learner support. For example, at the online learning insights Web site, there is a model for how to support online learners through their learning journey (Morrison, 2012).

For MOOCs, the team will need to decide what level of support you are able to provide, and to be clear and explicit with learners about what they can expect from you in terms of support. The level of academic support that is provided is one of the key decisions to make in designing the MOOC. This type of support is one of the key differentiators between face-to-face and virtual instruction, as there is a wide range of possible models for learner support, from none or very little, to one-to-one support. Experienced online providers put a great deal of time and effort into getting this right—and following through the student life cycle, from initial enquiry through application, studying, graduation, and continuing a relationship as an alumnus. For MOOCs, the typical approach is to provide limited academic support, usually within a one-to-many environment such as discussion forums, rather than individually. There is also an emphasis on using peer support, again through discussion forums, to discuss assignments and to answer queries. As was outlined in the case studies, some institutions provide additional support through volunteer or paid postgraduate students who monitor the relevant discussion forums, answer queries, and provide guidance.

It is essential to be realistic from the start about type of learner support that will be provided. Research that has been carried out in open and distance learning has identified ratios of about 25 students to 1 tutor as the minimum required in order to achieve good completion rates and these are the learner–tutor ratios that are used by the UK Open University and other distance learning providers (Tait, 2003). For a MOOC which has 5000 students registered, this would mean providing 200 tutors! Recent research by Diana Laurillard and colleagues has shown that it may be hard to exceed these ratios at present for learners studying online, notwithstanding the new tools and technologies that are available, unless you use a different pedagogic model: "The variable cost of high quality support *does not achieve economies of scale* if you maintain the same pedagogy" (Laurillard, 2013). We are not yet in the position where adaptive and personalized learning systems are sufficiently sophisticated to provide viable new models.

One of the typical models of MOOCs is to use other learners to support each other to interrogate and understand the learning materials, activity which is valuable in its own right, but research has shown that learners tend to do better with higher levels of support from academic specialists, and also that regular support from academic specialists can have a marked impact upon completion rates for MOOCs. You may instead need to consider whether there are other ways to support learners, such as by employing students or postgraduates as online teaching assistants, for example to monitor discussion boards and add academic input.

One of the difficult challenges presented by planning MOOCs is that you do not usually know your student numbers far in advance of running the course. So you may need to be able to scale your level of support up or down, depending on the number of registrations—and the number of registered students who actually participate in the course. In terms of administrative rather than academic support, this may include a generic e-mail address or discussion board to which enquiries can be addressed—in which case you need to be clear and explicit about response times that they can expect. You will need to ensure that administrative support staff are available to provide what is needed, and bear in mind that students are likely to be located in many different time zones, so may have expectations of support 24 h per day.

MOOC content and flipping the classroom

Interesting models are also developing for the use of MOOC content as part of a blended learning approach, where some or all of the content of a MOOC is used by an educational institution other than the one which developed it (Kolowich, 2013). In many cases, this is as part of a blended learning experience, where students access some or all of the MOOC content before they come into the classroom, they may carry out assignments, tests, and so on, and prepare materials before they meet for face-to-face contact with tutors and other students.

This is typical of the "flipped classroom" approach that has been much discussed in recent years—where engagement with learning materials takes place outside the classroom, in advance of classroom, seminar, tutorial, or laboratory time, rather than using face-to-face time in order to "transmit" information. Some would argue that this is not a new phenomenon and that the label is now at times being misused (Sams, 2011). It is obvious that in many disciplines, in particular the humanities, it is usual practice to require learners to engage deeply with reading materials and other resources outside the formal teaching situation. However, the flipped classroom debate has provided a helpful focus upon the value of using technology as part of a blended learning approach, and there is no doubt that the range of resources in many media that can now be made available to learners can provide different, and sometimes more accessible, attractive, or appropriate, ways for the learners to engage with concepts. It is particularly helpful to discuss the flipped classroom model when one of the developing MOOC models is for institutions to license content from other institutions and use it with their own students in a "flipped classroom" scenario.

To draw an obvious parallel: the use of a MOOC is similar to the approach that is taken to using text books as a key "course reader" or key text book. However, it can go much further than a text book because the student is able to engage with a richer set of materials in many different formats, and also to engage with other learners and tutors, in an informal and self-directed setting. There is almost unlimited potential to provide creative and new approaches to learning content through an online environment.

Conclusion

MOOCs are turning the traditional higher education proposition on its head, as they are allowing students to choose to learn from a huge range of different small, granular course offerings, rather than committing to a single institution and being limited to their courses. In order to compete in this new, more competitive and dynamic educational environment, it is essential that institutions understand more about the motivation of learners, in particular within the online environment. They also need to give careful and expert consideration to the design of the MOOC itself, drawing upon best practice. Current MOOC platforms may be limited in the media and learning design that they allow, but they will become more complex and sophisticated over time; and there are many other options for institutions to explore and include in experimental MOOC offerings, that can inform their choice of learning content and learning design for both online and blended learning experiences.

References

Beyond Distance Research Alliance. (2014). *The 7Cs of learning design toolkit.* Beyond Distance Research Alliance, Online at http://www2.le.ac.uk/projects/oer/oers/beyond-distance-research-alliance/7Cs-toolkit.

Conole, G. (2013a). *MOOCs as disruptive technologies: strategies for enhancing the learner experience and quality of MOOCs.* Eprints in Library and Information Science, Online at http://eprints.rclis.org/19388/.

Conole, G. (2013b). *Week 5: a new classification for MOOCs by Gráinne Conole.* European Foundation for Quality in E-learning, Online at http://mooc.efquel.org/a-new-classification-for-moocs-grainne-conole/.

Hartnett, M., St George, A., & Dron, J. (September 2011). Examining motivation in online distance learning environments: complex, multifaceted and situation-dependent. *The International Review of Research in Open and Distance Learning, 12*(6), 20–38. Online at http://www.irrodl.org/index.php/irrodl/article/view/1030/1954. ISSN 1492-3831.

Kolowich, D. (2013). 'In Deals With 10 Public Universities, Coursera Bids for Role in Credit Courses'. *The Chronicle of Higher Education.* Online at http://chronicle.com/article/In-Deals-With-10-Public/139533/.

Koper, R. (2006). Current research in learning design. *Educational Technology and Society, 9*(1), 13–22. Online at http://www.ifets.info/journals/9_1/3.pdf.

Laurillard, D. (2013). *Teaching as a Design Science.* Online and Open Access Learning in Higher Education. Observatory of Borderless Higher Education. Online at http://www.obhe.ac.uk/conferences/onlineopenaccs_london/MOOCs_S1_Laurillard.

Morrison, D. (2012). *Strategies for online instructors: Understanding the needs of the online learner.* Online Learning Insights, Online at http://onlinelearninginsights.wordpress.com/2012/08/20/strategies-for-online-instructors-understanding-the-needs-of-the-online-learner/.

Morrison, D. (2014). *Resources to help students be successful online in three areas: Technical, academic and study planning.* Online Learning Insights. https://onlinelearninginsights.wordpress.com/tag/supporting-online-learners/.

Sams, A. (2011). *Setting the flip straight.* The Daily Riff. http://www.thedailyriff.com/articles/the-flipped-class-shedding-light-on-the-confusion-critique-and-hype-801.php.

Tait, A. (2003). Reflections on student support in open and distance learning. *International Review of Research in Open and Distance Learning, 4*(1), 5.

Yuan, L., Powell, S., & Olivier, W. (2014). *Beyond MOOCs: Sustainable Online Learning in Institutions.* Centre for Educational Technology, Interoperability and Standards. Online at http://publications.cetis.ac.uk/2014/898.

Data and analytics

17

This chapter focuses upon data and analytics, which both have the potential to provide value to universities as they seek to reshape their offer and to differentiate themselves from their peers. So-called "big" data and analytics have been two of the hottest buzzwords in the technology press in recent years, and they have also received a lot of coverage in the business press more generally. Analytics is often considered as part of "big data," but is an area of research and development in its own right, as well as being used in many areas of the commercial world. It includes the analysis that is done to data in order to gain insights from it.

As with other technology-driven change, data and analytics hold the potential to both disrupt current business models and also to offer new opportunities, either for new products or for products to be adapted to new usage models. Used well, they may deliver benefits; but used badly, they may be costly and even potentially misleading or even damaging.

Big data is something of a catch-all term that has been somewhat overused in recent years, and misused to capture a whole set of different meanings. In this text, we will not discuss big data specifically, but instead focus upon educational data more generally—that is, the potential to gather and hold information about people, content, and other objects (such as software tools) in digital systems.

The obvious partner to data, then, is the analysis of these data—or more specifically, the new affordances of specialist analytic systems and tools, which have been designed to make it easier to interrogate and analyze the data in a meaningful and useful way.

Taken together, data and analytics have huge potential to offer added value to higher education providers, in particular when potentially working with students who are located away from the university ("virtual" students), and also when providing services to large numbers of students, such as through MOOCs, where Online learning and MOOCs, in particular, make it easier for universities to gather data about learning behaviour and learners.

It may seem that analytics is mostly about getting the right analysis tools and putting them into place. However, for many institutions the far greater challenges are the underlying data that are used to inform analysis, and the systems that hold the data. This is not a new challenge for universities; for many years, they have invested in developing information systems that are appropriate to external reporting requirements on student numbers and also developing appropriate financial and human resources systems. These long-term challenges are thrown into sharp relief, however, when the institution wishes to put analytics in place, in particular to carry out analysis of data that is held in a number of different places, and to carry out real-time analysis of it.

At Purdue University in the United States, acquiring the data that were needed to be able to carry out analysis was the biggest first hurdle in the implementation of the *Course Signals* analytics system: "our biggest difficulty was the acquisition of data. As a siloed university, different data were owned by different stewards, and compiling all the data needed for the student success algorithm was an uphill battle that took well over a year" (Pistilli, Arnold, & Bethune, 2012).

Purdue is not alone in perceiving that many of its data systems operate in separate silos; this is a common problem in other universities. Ownership of systems and the data in them adds an additional level of complexity; data systems have often been developed for a particular purpose, and the data are often perceived to be sensitive and in need of careful security protection, and these often-legitimate concerns can slow progress to implementation substantially. For this reason, it is important to get appropriate understanding of and buy-in to the MOOC development by management at all levels.

There is a need for clear institutional strategies and policies for MOOC data, in order to get greatest benefit from the investment in MOOCs; indeed, data about learners and their behavior are one of the benefits accrued through investment in MOOCs by institutions (Hollands & Terthali, 2014).

MOOCs and analytics

Analytics are of particular importance to MOOCs. There are characteristics of MOOCs that make it a very different experience to a traditional course delivery situation. Firstly, you do not know your students and because they have no formal relationship with the university, the usual ways that you might gather information about the student, through their interaction with various parts of the university, such as the library or student services, are not available to you. Secondly, the students are likely to join the course for a short period of time, perhaps 8 or 10 weeks in total, which minimizes still further the opportunities to build up a picture. Thirdly, you are likely to have far larger numbers of students taking the MOOC than you have on any other courses. This final point presents a big challenge, when you want to build up a picture of "how the students are doing," but also a significant opportunity, as there will be so many more students engaged with the materials, carrying out assessments, and so on, and so there are opportunities to build up significant quantities of data about the students, their learning behaviors, and so on.

So teachers are faced with a different situation than usual, one where the normal processes for eliciting student feedback will not be possible. Perhaps more importantly, there are exciting, new opportunities that emerge because there is a large cohort of students learning solely online, where their learning journey will create a trail of data as they progress. The teacher is able to find out much more about the students—who they are, why they joined the course, and even why they choose to leave—than they might do normally. Data that are gathered from online learning systems can also enable the teacher to get a much clearer picture than usual of how the students are progressing through the course, and so make it possible to identify where there are particular problem areas, where students behave differently than you expected, spending more or less time on an activity, for example. The teacher will be able to engage with discussions about course topics as they happen, and respond with guidance or extra resources. The data will come to the course team in "real time" as the course progresses, so they will be able to have a live picture of what is happening on the course, and respond to it, rather than waiting for the end of course evaluation. So one of the benefits of analytics, if used well, is that they can help course teams to design better courses and better learning environments for the students.

Those working at the cutting edge in the field of online education also have grander ambitions for how analytics can be used. Researchers at Stanford University, for example, hope that the rich source of data about how learners interact with materials online may lead to the development of much more sophisticated online learning environments, which may be able to adapt according to how the learner progresses, and particularly to help them with areas where they have difficulties. As researchers of how analytics can help the design of better MOOC experiences, their aim is to "provide educators, instructional designers, and platform developers with insights for designing effective and potentially adaptive learning environments that best meet the needs of MOOC participants" (Kizilcec, Piech, & Schnieder, 2013).

There is also the value that can be reaped from gathering data from courses that are repeated more frequently than usual—perhaps several times per year—to build up longitudinal pictures of key data such as the makeup of student populations, their previous interaction with the university, their progression through the materials, completion rates, and so on. Again, these data are not available for traditional courses but offer lots of possibilities for the institution to monitor course engagement much more closely than usual, and to make decisions about the institution's course offerings in a much more informed and responsive way.

Let us look at analytics more closely, both in terms of general online learning and in terms of MOOCs. Analytics has been used to support institutional strategies for a number of years and this experience can help to guide the use of analytics in MOOCs; in particular, in the support of strategies to help students and increase student retention (or completion). Innovative work is taking place in traditional teaching situations, where the results from analytic tools are used to guide interventions by teaching and support staff. At the University of Bolton in the UK, analytics is being used to drive face-to-face personal tutoring strategies as well as to help retention of students (Powell & MacNeill, 2012).

In the approach taken at the University of Bolton, analytic and information presentation tools, in the form of information dashboard, brings together data that would previously have been held in separate information silos, and possibly not interrogated at all.

In this example, the information provided is about the student's previous and current educational achievements, and the analytic tools automatically analyze the data and provide reports in order to highlight those students whom it predicted may do less well in their studies, or be at risk from dropping out early:

"An information dashboard allows staff, through a series of web-links, to access more detailed information about a student's attendance, and previous and current educational performance. An algorithm is used to highlight students most at risk of leaving the university, initially based on a combination of their UCAS points and attendance. As the student's career progresses, the UCAS data are replaced by data on their assessment outcomes in module examinations in an attempt to provide a more relevant snapshot of their likelihood of either leaving the university or performing poorly in assessments.

A weekly e-mail summarizes these data and is sent to relevant curriculum managers and personal tutors that flags students those are of concern using a traffic light system where red indicates urgent action is required" (Kraan & Sherlock, 2013).

Not all analytics traditions and tools are relevant to all areas where analytics might be applied. A business intelligence tool that is fine tuned for financial market predictive insights will be of limited use when analyzing student engagement in Virtual Learning Environment (VLE) forums, for example.

In the US, analytics have for several years been a key focus of innovation and development in both traditional education and e-learning systems, as issues of students completing their course are a particularly key concern for many institutions, and analytics are being applied in an attempt to improve the situation. The learning that has been gained from using analytics in both traditional learning and blended learning scenarios can be brought to bear in the MOOC context.

Purdue University has created its own *Course Signals* system, a real-time analytics system which is used to analyze data from a number of sources and to predict students' success with the course.

This example is of particular relevance to MOOCs as it applies to a context of gateway courses that are taken by large numbers of students who then wish to progress on to other courses at the university. In this situation, the teacher is not able to develop personal knowledge of the whole cohort and the students may be particularly challenged to build up their knowledge of an unfamiliar subject area and pass an assignment, with defined time constraints. This has some similarities with the MOOC context.

The *Course Signals* system uses data that is gathered in Purdue University's Course Management system (in this case, Blackboard) which monitors student interaction with the course materials and assignments. It analyzes the data and then gives the teacher a "traffic light" rating (red, yellow, or green) which indicates how likely the student is to pass the course. The teacher is then able to intervene by providing additional resources to the student or direct support. In one experiment, the system predicted that 66–80% of students might need additional support (Pistilli et al., 2012).

Research carried out in 2012 found that those students who were supported by the system did significantly better than others, with average grades higher and lower levels of dropout (Pistilli et al., 2012). Results so far also indicate that students who have been supported with *Signals* will graduate more quickly than their peers: "preliminary results suggest that Course Signals students graduate sooner, allowing them to enter the work world before many of their classmates" (Pistilli et al., 2012). If this trend continues, use of the *Course Signals* analytics system will be really significant for the University and the way that it supports its students.

Analytics in MOOCs

If we apply these kinds of approaches to a MOOC that is being run by a university, similar tools could be applied to try to predict which of the students are likely to complete or not, but the analytics system would need to be "fed" by different sources of data. The university is unlikely to have access to data about the student's prior academic achievements in any level of detail, for example, so for a MOOC, we may instead have to rely upon more usage data about what resources the student has accessed, and for how long, during their engagement with the MOOC material.

At present—and despite early promises—the MOOC systems that are widely used do not include sophisticated data analysis tools like *Course Signals*, or similar tools. In a recent presentation, the CEO of Coursera, Nancy Koller, described the current provision of Coursera data as "one big spreadsheet" (Koller, 2014). In the same presentation, Nancy Koller did however emphasize that both collection of data and analytic tools or data dashboards are a key priority for the development of the Coursera system (Koller, 2014).

There is real potential for those institutions that are able to understand more about their MOOC learners, either individually or as a whole population. Some of the key areas where analysis of data may provide value from MOOCs are described below. Note that these are just illustrative; there are likely to be many more opportunities for data analysis that arise as analytic tools become more sophisticated and as a particular institution builds up their own data set, and can look at patterns of data over time.

Key areas where universities may benefit from using data collection and analytics as part of their MOOC strategy are described below.

1. Student retention and completion of the course

Using analytics will help the university to understand the overall picture of how many students sign up for a MOOC, how many proceed through the course, and how many complete. If the right data are stored, it can also be analyzed at a more granular level to look at how many students have completed particular exercises.

If data can be stored about specific students, than as with the examples above, it can be used to predict future student behavior, for example to predict dropout by particular individuals. More likely, the behavior of the student population as a whole will help the course designers to think about how to design the course, and support activities, in order to keep more students and get them past key points during the course when dropout occurs, by understanding more about why people leave the course at particular points (see below).

2. Improving MOOC content

Analytic data can be used to help course designers to understand more about how the MOOC content is being used and then improve it. Two examples of how data may help to improve MOOCs are given below:

1. Understanding whether the learning design for the MOOC works—is there a particular point in the MOOC at which students leave the MOOC, and is it possible to establish why this is?

Is it because the MOOC has failed to engage students through boring or badly presented materials; whether the course description was misleading and so students have discovered that the course is not what they were expecting; or some other reason?

2. Identifying badly written or designed materials—for example, is there a particular assessment exercise which many learners fail or do not complete, and which may prove to be challenging to large numbers of students? In which case, can the course team plan an intervention, such as an additional support segment, to help students to understand the materials? If analysis is carried out during the course and regular reports produced for teaching and support staff, it may be possible to make these interventions during the course rather than at the end.

We need, however, to bear in mind that data and analytics can only take us so far in understanding the perceptions and behavior of students, and in attempting to predict future requirements and behaviors. Data are only as useful as the questions that are asked of it—and the tools that are applied to it. Although sophisticated analytic tools are available in other fields, in educational situations, the tools are still relatively unsophisticated, and there is little consistent practice that has taken place so far.

This is particularly the case for data in MOOCs, where the potential for analysis of data is still a long way from being fulfilled in reality. This is particularly the case for the large MOOC platforms, which gather immense amounts of data but at present do very little with it. As Hollands and Terthali (2014) note: "while there is no doubt that the MOOC platforms collect oceans of data, it is apparent that interpreting these data and querying them … is a work in progress."

The difficulty seems to be that the major platforms have planned to collect data from the use of MOOCs, but did not consider in advance the analytical questions that universities might want to ask of the data. The data that are stored is that which is automatically stored for any Web site, not specifically for educational purposes. So the data are largely unstructured and may be stored in separate files, and a lot of additional work is needed in order to draw useful conclusions from it. Hollands and Terthali give the example of a researcher who is trying to analyze the user data from some edX MOOCs to find out what percentage of the learning materials had been read by each student, in order to inform the future design of the MOOC. This query is one which we might expect to be fairly commonplace, but in this case, it could not be answered without the researcher carrying out a great deal of bespoke, and time-consuming analysis of the data by designing and running their own computational queries using a programming language. The report estimates that it took 9 months of a computer scientist's time to create and conduct this and other standard queries that were needed to carry out standard data analysis of a single MOOC (Hollands & Terthali, 2014).

So although the MOOC platforms promise much for the data that are collected, the reality is likely to be very different. In the case studies that were carried out, universities reported planning to carry out their own additional analysis of the data that were returned to them by the MOOC platforms, but that this substantial undertaking had not yet taken place and was subject to investment of human resources into specific local information systems and their own sets of queries.

In summary, it is perhaps most accurate to say that the data collection and analysis tools are not yet sufficiently mature to be easily applied to standard queries about learner behavior in MOOCs, so institutions need to plan additional local manipulation of the data.

There are two other, specific issues to consider related to analytics and data storage and management.

- Data ownership, privacy, and rights issues

All data that are created by tracking the behavior of users of the MOOC materials is subject to complex data ownership, privacy and rights' issues. For those institutions that are working with a third-party MOOC platform rather than collecting and storing data locally, this is more complex, as they are likely to be subject to privacy laws and rights issues in more than one domain. We recommend that the university's legal team is consulted before learner data is collected or analyzed, and also before access to the data by third parties is permitted, and that full consideration is also given to the ethical issues of using learner data in ways with which participants may not be familiar (Neal, 2014).

- The limitations of "hard" data

Though we advise that part of the MOOC strategy should address the issue of data and analytics, it is important to bear in that there are limits to what can be concluded from the collection and interrogation of "hard" data. Particularly given the difficulties reported above in conducting even simple queries, it is important not to be drawn into a belief that data and analytic reports can provide all the answers to questions such as: how successful is the MOOC? Who is using it and what are they learning? What works well and what does not?

A strategy for the qualitative analysis of user perceptions needs to be put in place alongside the strategy for data and analytics, as part of the overall evaluation strategy, as previously discussed. As recent research has shown, for example, two similar populations of MOOC students, studying the same materials, can achieve very different results from the same assessments (Halawa, 2014). All "hard" data need to be complemented and informed by qualitative data, such as data from interviews, focus groups, and user diaries. This should be considered as part of the MOOC strategy.

References

Halawa, S., Greene, D., & Mitchell, J. (2014). *Dropout Prediction in MOOCs using Learner Activity Features*. Proceedings of the European MOOC Summit (EMOOCs 2014), Feb 10-12, 2014, Lausanne, Switzerland, Online at http://web.stanford.edu/~halawa/cgi-bin/files/emoocs2014.pdf.

Hollands, F. M., & Terthali, D. (2014). *MOOCs: Expectations and reality*. Educause, Online at http://www.educause.edu/library/resources/moocs-expectations-and-reality.

Kizilcec, R. F., Piech, C., & Schnieder, E. (2013). *Deconstructing disengagements: Analyzing learner subpopulations in massive open online courses*. ACM, Online at http://www.stanford.edu/~cpiech/bio/papers/deconstructingDisengagement.pdf.

Koller, N. (2014). The online revolution: education for everyone. In *Paper presented at the university college access lecture, 17 June 2014, at the T.S.Eliot lecture theatre*. University of Oxford.

Kraan, W., & Sherlock, D. (2013). Analytics tools and infrastructure *CETIS analytics series* (Vol. 1). No.11. CETIS. Online at http://publications.cetis.ac.uk/wp-content/uploads/2013/01/Analytics-Tools-and-Infrastructure-Vol-1-No11.pdf.

Neal, C. (2014). *MOOCs lead to massive data collection*. The Heartland Institute, Online at http://news.heartland.org/newspaper-article/2014/12/20/moocs-lead-massive-data-collection.

Pistilli, M. D., Arnold, K., & Bethune, M. (2012). *Signals: Using academic analytics to promote student success*. Educause Review Online, Online at http://www.educause.edu/ero/article/signals-using-academic-analytics-promote-student-success.

Powell, S., & MacNeill, S. (2012). Institutional readiness for analytics *CETIS analytics series* (Vol. 1). No.8. CETIS. Online at http://publications.cetis.ac.uk/wp-content/uploads/2012/12/Institutional-Readiness-for-Analytics-Vol1-No8.pdf.

The developing MOOC market

18

Although the business models are not yet clear and income generation is unproven, there is a huge amount of interest in the possibilities of Massive Open Online Courses (MOOCs) to take part of the traditional higher education market, and also, potentially, to create new markets—that is, to attract new "customers" to higher education, or to offer new higher education products to existing customers.

We have seen unbundling of services taking place in other marketplaces over the last two decades, and seen dramatic change in some industries, as traditional providers of products and services have specialized their provision, and outsourced sets of products and services, where they can be provided more effectively and efficiently by others.

To date, higher education has been a fairly closed and restricted market, which has largely escaped this move to unbundle and specialize. This is because accreditation of higher education qualifications has been restricted to specific providers rather than open to a competitive market, by providing most of the requisite facilities and services themselves, rather than through third-parties. With notable exceptions, such as some of the private providers, most universities have provided a bundle of different products or services, ranging from accommodation for students, to leisure facilities, tuition, examinations, and accreditation. Many markets have become increasingly specialist and have provided smaller bundles of services from a single provider, but higher education providers have often moved in the other direction and have increased or enhanced the services that they provide. Particularly in the United States, this approach is used to justify a significant price tag for a whole higher education "experience" with universities that have a similar offer in terms of quality of academic provision and similar rankings in league tables, competing on the basis of "extras" such as climbing walls and fancy swimming pools.

However, as the scalability of Internet technology impacts upon higher education provision, and we see different products—like online- and distance-learning courses, and MOOCs—emerge, the higher education product is also beginning to unbundle in some cases, and there is the potential for a range of service providers to enter the marketplace and provide some of the services to universities. We saw some examples of this in the case studies, where universities are working with third-party providers of examinations under invigilation conditions. In online- and distance-learning, student recruitment may commonly be provided by a specialist, third-party organization.

As we have discussed, MOOCs are an immature and unproven product and their market is unknown and unclear, so it may seem strange that profit-making organizations are keen to enter into the MOOC market as fast as possible. Demographics, with a growing market of young people seeking higher education and whose demand is not currently being met, and the opening up of previously restricted markets, by allowing some new entrants to grant credit, probably explains the rush to offer higher education products.

Below, we will describe some of the new entrants, and main competitors, entering into the higher education market through the use of Internet technologies.

For-profit online providers of higher education

The obvious competitors to traditional providers of higher education are the online and for-profit higher education providers that have appeared in recent decades, with mixed levels of success. Companies such as the University of Phoenix, Laureate, and Kaplan have become familiar international brands, either providing the full range of higher education services themselves or working through partner organizations, particularly with traditional universities. While the reputation of some of the independent, for-profit universities has been damaged by high dropout rates and sometimes poor quality assurance, providers of unbundled services working in partnership with existing institutions seem to be more successful and growing relatively quickly.

In the United Kingdom, for example, the University of Liverpool has for a number of years worked with the for-profit company, Laureate, to provide "the University of Liverpool Online," which offers 100% distance-learning postgraduate degree courses to many students each year. In this particular example, the University provides accreditation and academic credibility, while Laureate provides a large bundle of different services—marketing and recruitment of students, administrative services, and also provides the technical platform, and supports the creation of quality-assured learning resources and even tuition of students. The University provides accreditation of the academic qualifications, and perhaps most importantly, the internationally recognized brand that helps to attract students, parents and others to consider the University of Liverpool Online to be credible enough for them to invest in for their futures.

There are a number of companies that provide some parts of the student experience lifecycle. Companies such as Academic Partnerships and Embanet Compass will offer a flexible range of different services to their university partner or customer, from market research and recruitment services, to technology services (like hosting content), through to student-facing services, such as support and even student retention, but also providing some aspects of "academic" services, such as course development and even training of academic staff. This level of unbundling begins to seriously blur the boundary between the university experience that is provided by the university itself and that which comes from its expert provider or partner. It is a controversial area, and the issues are not clear cut.

The MOOC freemium model can offer a potential value to providers of higher education services, offering as it does a way to cut through traditional market share and offer possible customers the opportunity to sample their product directly and at no cost. These types of companies are also interested in the freemium.

Publishers

Both educational and mainstream publishers are likely to be interested in MOOCs and their future, both as a threat and as an opportunity. As a threat, because MOOCs seem to go further support the model that quality content is available for free from the Internet. As an opportunity, because by using an educational model that focuses upon content delivery through technology rather than through the use of physical campuses, MOOCs may open up the marketplace for other providers of content to compete with universities. The possible unbundling of the university "products" and its potential to open up provision to a broader range of service providers has been much discussed in recent years, in particular in the report "An Avalanche is Coming" (Rizvi et al., 2013) and Bacow, Bowen, Guthrie, Lack, and Long (2012).

As we have discussed, unbundling offers the potential to break up of the traditional university product into a number of different possible services or offers. Organizations like publishers have experience of owning, or acquiring rights to, huge amounts of academic content, and repackaging it to create new products. As the university product is increasingly delivered in a virtual form, it becomes much easier for a content owner to provide parts of the experience. In addition, organizations such as Pearson offer other steps in the educational life cycle, such as certified testing services for examinations, and a network of bricks-and-mortar testing centers. Hardly surprising that Pearson has already teamed up with various university MOOC providers to partner in pilot projects that involve following informal participation in MOOCs online with formal testing at accredited test centers (Pearson, 2013).

So we see that the unbundling of higher education offers opportunities for organizations like publishers who have traditionally provided some pieces of the traditional university offer, to refocus or even expand their offer. And this is not just about understanding how to acquire, manage, and disseminate academic content; publishers are also able to use their expertise in managing and analyzing huge amounts of digital data, offering "added value" services of data analysis or analytics. It is no coincidence, for example, that Houghton Mifflin Harcourt recently bought an "educational solutions" company, Chapters, which provides learning portfolios and accreditation services, and announced a partnership with Knewton, one of the leading adaptive learning companies—in total, providing many of the components that will potentially provide a personalized and adaptive learning experience.

Software and systems service providers

As discussed above, many industries have seen a breaking down of their traditional products into smaller services, with a number of different companies specializing in providing parts of the product life cycle or pipeline. This approach means that new entrants are able to offer specific and tailored services to higher education, and also to cross the traditional boundaries to provide some of the services that the bricks-and-mortar university would traditionally have to provide for itself.

Over the last 20 years, we have seen the growth of companies, such as Blackboard (the most popular Learning Management System in higher education), providing products that universities use to manage digital educational content and interaction with learners. As content management has increasingly moved into a cloud-based model with content (and increasingly applications) stored and managed on specialist systems that are remote from the content creator, software providers are also able to provide parts of the IT-enabled higher education system.

We have seen the "move to the cloud" has impacted upon the provision of local university IT services, such as email and storage. In this scenario, the systems are sold to the University as a service, rather than the University buying, hosting, and maintaining its own, local implementation of software. The university may increasingly buy specialist services, such as plagiarism detection, from a range of different providers, rather than buying one set of IT systems from a single provider.

As discussed in the previous chapter, the use of IT systems to underpin parts of the education system also brings with it the potential to store, manage, and analyze educational data of all kinds, in ways that have never before been possible. There are new opportunities for specialist companies such as Knewton to build upon their product and provide services that have not been possible before, such as predictive testing of academic ability, and truly personalized, individualized educational systems—and many are well aware of the potential benefits that this may bring to their market share—see the views expressed by the CEO of Knewton, Jose Ferreira (2014).

Implications for universities in the future

So we can see that the higher education market has the potential to become much more volatile and to include a much wider range of possible service providers, and possible partners, than was previously the case. As the virtual delivery of some of the services of the university becomes widespread, the university product will in some cases begin to "unbundle." So what does this mean for current universities?

On one hand, there are positive possibilities inherent in a model where the university can choose to buy the "best of breed" service or product from a third party. Where providers specialize in the creation of particular parts of the university product, there is potential to offer a better service to students, potentially with greater personalization, and more choice. It may be possible to offer degrees at a lower cost if the university is able to buy in services in a more flexible way, buying what they need and when they need it, rather than having to build and own everything for themselves. However, this is the promise and not yet the reality for many parts of the university life cycle; buying in services may lead to less choice and poorer quality of service to the student. Experience to date with providers of some online, cloud-based services is not wholly positive. There are also issues with sensitive data, such as personal information, being stored and managed by external companies.

There is no doubt, though, that the greatest amount of innovation is likely to take place in companies that are trying to create new, competitive higher education products. Universities are advised to monitor change closely and to make purchasing—and partnership—decisions based upon the current and planned expertise of their current and possible future providers.

What is also clear is that the unbundling of the university product, at the same time as demographic changes and changes to accreditation, means that the higher education market is opening up to new entrants. Universities are advised to closely monitor changes in the higher education marketplace and to seek out the right partnerships and opportunities that will help them to achieve their strategy, making the best use of expertise from new and specialist providers as appropriate. They may need to seek out new sources of expertise and develop new skillsets in their staff, to make the most of the opportunities that will arise over the next 10 years. MOOCs provide one, lower risk way to experimenting with new partnerships and models of delivery.

References

Bacow, L. S., Bowen, W. G., Guthrie, K. M., Lack, K. A., & Long, M. P. (2012). *Barriers to adoption of online learning systems in U. S. higher education*. Ithaka S&R, Online at http://www.sr.ithaka.org/research-publications/barriers-adoption-online-learning-systems-us-higher-education.

Ferreira, J. (2014). *The unbundling of higher education*. Knewton, Online at http://www.knewton.com/blog/ceo-jose-ferreira/unbundling-higher-education/.

Pearson. (2013). *edX announces option of proctored exam testing through collaboration with Pearson VUE*. Pearson, Online at http://www.pearsonvue.com/about/release/archive/12_09_06_edx.asp.

Rizvi, S., Donnelly, K., & Barber, M. (2013). *An Avalanche is Coming. Higher education and the revolution ahead*. Institute for Public Policy Research, Online at http://www.ippr.org/publications/an-avalanche-is-coming-higher-education-and-revolution-ahead.

Appendix A

Understanding your MOOC-i-vation

The six case studies focus upon the strategic imperative, or motivation, for universities to engage with MOOCs. We have focused upon the distinctive characteristics of that imperative to describe each case study.

It is useful to think about the strategic perspective that your institution has on MOOCs before you design your strategy.

The six perspectives included are:

1. the old hands

Characteristics:

- You take an institution-wide approach to online and distance learning
- You have experience of running fee-charged online courses

2. the opportunists

Characteristics:

- universities that have spotted the potential to use MOOCs to gain specific strategic advantage for their institution, without necessarily making long-term commitment to them

3. the confident entrepreneurs

- those who are investing heavily in MOOCs and leading the way in shaping the MOOC-scape

4. the institutional innovators—those who are investing in MOOCs as part of a holistic strategy for institutional innovation

5. the cautious

- those who are dipping their toe in the water but not willing to take risk or invest heavily;

6. the old guard

- the elite institutions that are circumspect about investment in any innovation, including MOOCs.

Appendix B

Checklist of costs for developing MOOCs

Budget item	Estimated cost per MOOC ($, euro, or £)
1. Market research—understanding your target audience 2. MOOC design 3. Content creation 4. Copyright assurance and clearance 5. Legal advice 6. Technical infrastructure 7. Management costs—project management 8. Quality assurance 9. Evidence-based improvement (evaluation, etc.) 10. Governance 11. (a) Additional costs that are specific to in-house MOOCs (platform costs, etc.) Or 11. (b) Additional costs that are incurred by working with partner platforms 12. Publicity and marketing 13. Other costs incurred Total:	

Appendix C

Framework for the design and evaluation of MOOCs, Lytics Lab, Stanford University

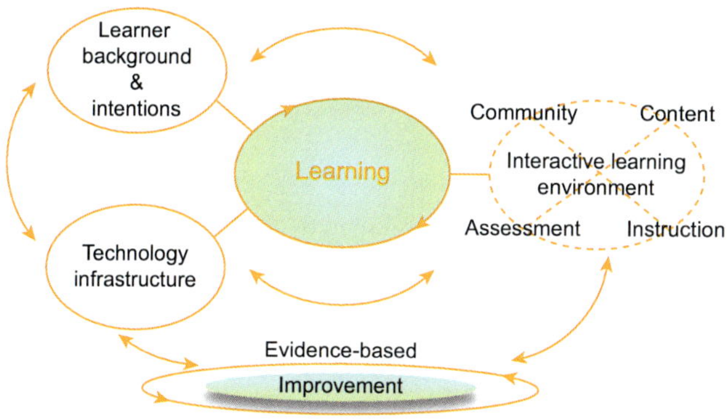

This framework provides a model to describe the context in which the MOOC is being designed, run, and evaluated. It is useful because it gives us a sense of the range of factors that are involved in designing and running the MOOC.

It has four main components: learner background and intentions; technology infrastructure; interactive learning environment (ILE), and evidence-based improvement.

"The *Interactive Learning Environment (ILE)* is made up of the core course elements—*Content*, *Instruction* (or Pedagogy), *Assessment*, and *Community*. These elements are initially shaped by the course creators as well as the technical affordances of the course platform. These design choices reflect the assumptions of designers about the ways in which people learn, and should be pushed to reflect the state of the art of knowledge in the learning sciences. …

Learner background and intention captures the variety of learner purposes for course engagement, which is a by-product of the open access nature of the courses and the novelty of the medium. Based on surveys we have conducted in some MOOCs, in addition to traditional students taking the course for some form of credit, a large percentage of others are enrolled with purposes as assorted as "curiosity about the topic," "to sharpen my job skills," and "fun and challenge." This pattern implies a need to serve up different courses suited to the varied purposes of MOOC learners: a customized learning approach that could be enabled by analytics on behavioral data from learners, as well as self-reported intentions for MOOC enrollment. …

The *technology infrastructure* comprising the MOOC platform used in conjunction with social media and other technology tools for augmenting communication and interaction powers the MOOC as a whole including its learning analytics engine, and serves to cater to diverse learner needs ranging from geography and language to issues of how the MOOC content is accessed and interacted with (e.g., downloading vs streaming video). …

Evidence-based improvement is a meta-MOOC process undergirding design decisions around the ILE and technology infrastructure. Evidence-based improvement is powered by data mining and analytics designed to measure the desired course learning outcomes, and incorporates qualitative evidence from sources like forums and surveys" (Grover et al., 2013).

Index

Note: Page numbers followed by "f" and "t" indicate figures and tables respectively.

Edwards Brothers Malloy
Thorofare, NJ USA
May 12, 2015